The Lighter Side of Soups

CLASSIC TOMATO SOUP
• PAGE 19 •

PUMPKIN SOUP
• PAGE 30 •

ZUCCHINI & SPINACH SOUP
• PAGE 25 •

WATERMELON GAZPACHO
• PAGE 40 •

PETITE PEA SOUP
• PAGE 29 •

BIG-BATCH VEGETABLE SOUP
• PAGE 43 •

IRISH CABBAGE SOUP
• PAGE 45 •

LEMON CHICKEN SOUP
• PAGE 75 •

DIJON VEGETABLE CHOWDER
• PAGE 46 •

ITALIAN TORTELLINI-SAUSAGE SOUP
• PAGE 76 •

JAPANESE SOBA SOUP
• PAGE 49 •

RICE CONGEE SOUP
• PAGE 77 •

SOUPE AU PISTOU
• PAGE 59 •

TORTILLA CHICKEN SOUP
• PAGE 79 •

ASIAN CHICKEN NOODLE SOUP
• PAGE 81 •

CIOPPINO
• PAGE 104 •

SALMON CHOWDER
• PAGE 96 •

THAI HOT & SOUR SOUP
• PAGE 105 •

TUNISIAN AROMATIC FISH SOUP
• PAGE 99 •

PHO BO
• PAGE 127 •

SPANISH SEAFOOD SOUP
• PAGE 101 •

SMOKY CHILI-BEEF SOUP
• PAGE 128 •

ASIAN BEEF NOODLE SOUP
• PAGE 130 •

KAMUT & CHICKPEA SOUP
• PAGE 150 •

RUSTIC SAUSAGE SOUP
• PAGE 139 •

TUSCAN FARRO & BEAN SOUP
• PAGE 155 •

SWEDISH YELLOW SPLIT-PEA SOUP
• PAGE 141 •

SOUTHWESTERN BLACK BEAN & RICE SOUP
• PAGE 163 •

PASTA E FAGIOLI
• PAGE 146 •

RISOTTO PRIMAVERA SOUP
• PAGE 167 •

ENLIGHTENED Soups

Also by Camilla V. Saulsbury

Cookie Dough Delights

Brownie Mix Bliss

Cake Mix Cookies

No-Bake Cookies

Puff Pastry Perfection

Panna Cotta

Enlightened Chocolate

Enlightened Cakes

ENLIGHTENED
Soups

More than 135 Light, Healthy, Delicious, and
Beautiful Soups in 60 Minutes or Less

CAMILLA V. SAULSBURY

CUMBERLAND HOUSE
NASHVILLE, TENNESSEE

ENLIGHTENED SOUPS
PUBLISHED BY CUMBERLAND HOUSE PUBLISHING, INC.
431 Harding Industrial Drive
Nashville, TN 37211

Cover design: JulesRulesDesign
Text design: Lisa Taylor

ISBN 978-1-58182-664-7 (hardcover)
Printed in the U.S.A.

"I LIVE ON GOOD SOUP, NOT ON FINE WORDS."

—MOLIÈRE

CONTENTS

ENLIGHTENED
Soups

INTRODUCTION

IF ONE FOOD CONJURES UP COMFORT, it is homemade soup. A dose of serenity sipped from a spoon, soup is as comforting as home itself.

Homemade soup also comes close to being the perfect meal: easy to make, naturally low in fat, rich with nutrients, convenient, and economical, it is a superfood from most every perspective.

In addition, recent studies indicate that eating a healthful soup produces greater feelings of satisfaction and satiety at meals than a variety of other types of food. Researchers aren't sure why, but speculate that it may have to do with soup's high water content, as well as the piping hot serving temperature, which slows down the speed of eating, allowing time to notice a feeling a fullness.

The primary reasons that you'll want to make each and every soup in this collection, though, are simple. First, they are absolutely and unfailingly delicious. Second, they are loaded with healthful ingredients, with a minimum of fat and calories. And third, they are all easy to make in 60 minutes or less.

My recipes honor the classics but tweak tradition enough to keep them healthful and fresh, making all of these soups modern favorites as well as tried-and-true friends. Think Lemon Chicken Soup with Fresh Spinach & Pasta, Roasted Vegetable Minestrone, Italian Tortellini-Sausage Soup, Summer Corn & Basil Bisque, and Split-Pea Soup with Caramelized Onions.

I've also researched a wealth of soups from across the country and around the world, then adapted them to make them healthier and home-cook friendly. Some examples are Tunisian Chickpea Soup, Tuscan Farro & Bean Soup, West African Peanut Soup, and Thai Chicken & Coconut Soup. I've tried to bring you the world in a bowl, one sip and slurp at a time.

It won't take much time or effort to work your way through these recipes because soup-making has an honest minimalism that makes it accessible and appealing to home cooks of every level of ability. I've simplified things further by creating the recipes with particularly straightforward cooking techniques and easy-to-find ingredients, and then categorizing each according to total preparation and cooking time: 20, 30, 45, or 60 minutes.

Finally, all of my recipes are well tested and follow recognized "enlightened" guidelines for healthy eating, including no more than 10 grams of fat per serving and utilization of healthy fats and oils, lean meats, and plenty of vegetables. In other words, each recipe delivers contentment on multiple fronts.

So pull out the pots and pans. For ever-pleasing soups equally at home in the dining room or kitchen, you need look no further than *Enlightened Soups*, because fast, healthful, delicious soup is always in style. Soup's on!

TOP 10 TIPS FOR ENLIGHTENED SOUPS

Whether you're making Classic Tomato Soup, Garden Gazpacho, or Rice Congee Soup, it helps to remember that soup is a forgiving dish, making it one of the best ways to experience the magic of cooking. Soup offers the opportunity to learn about the fundamentals of cooking, from sautéing to caramelizing to the blending of techniques, textures, and flavors, all with easy-to-follow steps. Further, soup is flexible, meaning you can tweak it to your palate's content.

Nevertheless, it's always important to begin by reading through the recipe, checking that you have all the necessary ingredients, and then gathering all the needed equipment for the task.

And for even greater assurance of success, follow my top ten tips for enlightened soup-making:

1. Know Your Salt & Pepper

Proper seasoning with salt and pepper is the key difference between a great soup and a humdrum soup. Salt is about as close to a magic ingredient as there is. Proper seasoning with salt doesn't make a soup salty; rather, the myriad complex flavors of the brew come to the fore. But add too much, and all your hard work can be ruined.

To keep this from occurring in your kitchen, follow this technique: When seasoning with salt to taste near the end of cooking, get in the habit of using your fingertips instead of a shaker. Simply place the salt in your palm or a small dish and pinch a small amount into the soup. This method allows far greater control of the salt added to the pot and will also help you develop a tactile knowledge of how much is just the right amount.

If you do over-salt your soup, there's still hope: Cut up a raw potato or two and drop it into the mix. It will absorb some of the salt and make the soup more edible.

Fresh peppercorns are likewise key to creating great soup. They have tremendous flavor, especially when compared to the preground stuff. You can use your own pepper grinder or look for the new peppercorn bottles in the supermarket with the grinder built in.

2. Cut the Fat in the Sauté Step

Many soup recipes, including the ones I've developed here, begin by cooking and stirring aromatic vegetables—onions, garlic, peppers, ginger—in butter or oil. These basic mixtures go by different names in different cuisines—a French *mirepoix*, an Italian *soffritto*, or a Portuguese *refogado*—but they all provide a foundation of flavor to the finished soup.

But while more traditional recipes call for multiple tablespoons—even ½ cup or more—of fat, the soups in this collection rely on 1 or 2 teaspoons or tablespoons, at most. The results are still delicious (the vegetables are softened and slightly caramelized), and the technique can be applied to other soups in your repertoire. (Note that if the vegetables stick a bit, simply add a small amount of broth or water to the pan.)

3. Don't Go Stir Crazy

In the first phase of cooking the soup (i.e., cooking and stirring the onions, aromatics, and other vegetables), don't stir the vegetables too often; once every two minutes or so is plenty. This helps them brown, caramelizing their sugars. That, in turn, will further enhance the flavor of the soup without adding excess fat.

4. Purée Soup in Blenders, in Small Batches

When making puréed soups, use a blender for the creamiest texture. A food processor will give a slightly grainy texture. Handheld immersion blenders are excellent when you only want to blend soups a little bit, but they are not effective for making creamy purées.

Be sure to purée in small batches and crack the blender lid slightly (or remove the center cap from the lid). **Steam can build up once you start blending, and if the lid is on tight or the blender is overfilled, it will spray hot soup all over you and your kitchen.** For protection, cover the top with a dishtowel while puréeing.

5. Steer Clear of High Heat

As one who has scorched her fair share of soups in days gone by, I urge you to consider the following: Keep the burner dial away from HIGH, even when bringing soup to a boil. It can take mere seconds for a soup to scorch if left unattended, boiling on high heat.

6. Handle Dairy Additions with Care

Follow the directions carefully for adding dairy products to soup. Keep the heat relatively low to prevent the dairy product from separating; boiling will create an unpleasant texture. Most soups in this collection call for the addition of any dairy products at the very end of cooking, with no more than a few minutes of gentle heating to warm completely.

And if you're making a soup ahead of time, prepare it up to the point of adding the dairy, then cool and store. Reheat the soup when you're ready to eat, adding the dairy for quick heating just before serving.

7. Give Yourself Permission to Use Ready-Prepped Ingredients

Sure, fresh is best. But when you're exhausted and hungry, my position is that a home-made soup made with a few shortcuts is still so much better—both in terms of taste and good health—than fast food. So go head and plan for those emergency moments. Check out my list of pantry ideas, but also consider stocking up on frozen chopped onions and peppers, frozen diced potatoes (stocked with the hash browns in the supermarket freezer case), and minced jarred garlic for those times when you're too pooped to peel and chop. And don't forget pregrated Parmesan cheese, prewashed greens, presliced mushrooms, and chopped vegetables from the supermarket salad bar, too.

8. Cut Vegetables Small for Faster Cooking

A ½-inch-size chop or dice needs no more than 10 minutes of simmering before it's soft, speeding soup to the table in no time.

9. Head to the Deli Counter for Cooked Meat and Poultry

You don't need to simmer meat and poultry for hours on end to pack healthy, flavorful protein into soup. Head to the deli counter of your supermarket for a wide selection of fully cooked meats. Shred the meat from deli rotisserie chicken (discard the skin and freeze any leftover meat for future meals), or request thick cuts of roast beef, smoked turkey, and ham, then dice into small pieces at home. Because the meat and poultry are fully cooked, they only need a few minutes of warming in the final phases of cooking.

10. Add Instant Dazzle with a Drizzle, Splash, or Sprinkle

Elevate any enlightened soup, whether for everyday or entertaining, with a sprinkle or drizzle of one of the following: a few shavings of Parmesan cheese made with a vegetable peeler, flavorful oil (extra-virgin olive oil, hazelnut oil, toasted sesame oil), finely grated citrus zest, or ready-made condiments such as black olive tapenade, sun-dried tomato tapenade, or basil pesto. A small splash of citrus juice (lemon or lime), red wine vinegar, cider vinegar, or good-quality balsamic vinegar can brighten and enhance the flavors of many soups, too.

Stocking your pantry with healthy basics is the solution for facing the perfect storm of culinary crises: you're hungry, it's late, and the refrigerator looks bare. Having great staples at the ready in the pantry, refrigerator, and freezer—things that will stay good for months on end like low-sodium broth, canned beans, pasta, and frozen vegetables—insures that a delicious and healthy soup is never more than minutes away. Here are some of my suggestions:

Dry Goods

Broths: Ready made, low-sodium broth is the essential foundation for almost every recipe in this collection.

While a wide range of good-quality options exist, I am most partial to Swanson® brand certified organic broths. All of the recipes in this collection were tested with this brand of broth. It is available in chicken, beef, and vegetable. In addition to being organic, it is also all natural, low sodium, MSG free, 99% fat free, and the chicken and beef varieties are made from chicken and cattle raised without hormones or antibiotics. From a busy home cook's perspective, I also appreciate that it is available at most grocery stores.

Whichever brand of broth you choose, look for the handy paper cartons, which are typically packaged in 32-ounce, 48-ounce, and occasionally 16-ounce sizes. Once opened, they can be stored in the refrigerator for up to 1 week.

Canola Oil: Pressed from rapeseed, canola oil is a neutral-flavored vegetable oil that is extremely low in saturated fat and quite high in monounsaturated fat. It is used extensively throughout this collection.

Olive Oil: Olive oil is monounsaturated oil that is prized for a wide range of cooking preparations, including soups. For the recipes in this collection, I recommend plain olive oil (the products are labeled simply olive oil); it contains a combination of refined olive oil and virgin or extra-virgin olive oil. It has a mild flavor and is significantly less expensive than extra-virgin olive oil.

Extra-virgin olive oil is the result of the first pressing of cold-pressed olives and is considered the finest and fruitiest of the olive oils. Its delicate, fruity nuances break down during cooking and simmering, making the added expense a waste. It's best to reserve it for a final drizzle atop individual servings of soups, or for other purposes altogether.

Canned Tomatoes: Canned tomatoes may sound nutritionally benign (if not bereft), but nothing could be further from the truth. Unlike some other canned vegetables, canned tomatoes retain almost all of their nutrients (they actually contain more lycopene than raw tomatoes). Very high in vitamins C and A, canned tomatoes are also a time-crunched cook's best friend. They are available in various forms, including peeled, whole, crushed, and those with herbs such as oregano and/or basil added. Keep multiple cans on hand for instant dinners.

Tomato paste: Tomato paste is made from tomatoes that have been cooked for several hours, then strained and reduced to a deep red, richly flavored concentrate. Just a tablespoon or two can greatly enrich ready-made broth, making it taste like it has been slow-cooking for hours. Look for it both in cans and tubes.

Marinara sauce: Jarred marinara sauce—a highly seasoned Italian tomato sauce made with onions, garlic, basil, and oregano—is typically used on pasta and meat, but it is also a great pantry staple for creating a delicious soup in mere minutes. For example, combine a jar with a small amount of chicken or vegetable broth, a few cooked vegetables and cooked pasta, and you have a delectable pasta-vegetable soup. Choose varieties with minimal ingredients and extra flavorings for the most versatility.

Chunky salsa: Like marinara sauce, ready-made chunky salsa—rich with tomatoes, peppers, onions, and spices but low in calories—instantly packs tremendous flavor into quick soups. Stir it directly into soup to thicken or enrich the broth, or dollop it atop the finished soup for added flavor.

Canned beans: Beans are legumes, dating back at least 4,000 years, and are among the oldest foods known to humans. Their high protein content, along with the fact that they're so readily available and inexpensive, makes them ideal for a wide range of quick and healthy soups. Be sure to drain and rinse them (unless otherwise directed) before adding to soup. I recommend keeping the following varieties on hand:

* Black beans
* White beans (e.g., cannellini and white navy beans)
* Pinto beans
* Kidney beans
* Black-eyed peas
* Garbanzo beans (chickpeas)

Canned seafood: Keeping a few cans and pouches of seafood in the pantry is a healthy and delicious way to add flavor and protein to a variety of healthy soups. It's an inexpensive and easy-to-prepare source of important nutrients like omega-3, calcium, proteins, and more. I recommend keeping the following varieties on hand:

* Shrimp (tiny or medium)
* Lump crabmeat
* Oysters

Evaporated Fat-Free Milk: Produced by evaporating nearly half the water from fresh fat-free milk, this thick milk product is an excellent option for replacing heavy cream in a wide range of soups.

Canned Light Coconut Milk: Coconut milk is a readily available and very affordable product made by combining equal parts water and shredded fresh or desiccated coconut meat and simmering until foamy. The light varieties have 75 percent less fat than regular coconut milk. While the consistency is not as thick, it is perfect in soups, and the flavor is still superb. It works particularly well in Asian, Central American, and Caribbean-inspired soups.

Dried Spices

All of the recipes in this book use ground, as opposed to whole, spices. Freshness is everything with ground spices. The best way to determine if a ground spice is fresh is to open the container and smell it. If it still has a strong fragrance, it is acceptable for use. If not, toss it and make a new purchase. I recommend keeping the following spices on hand for a wide range of soups:

* Allspice
* Cayenne pepper
* Cinnamon
* Chili powder
* Chipotle chile powder
* Cardamom
* Coriander
* Cumin
* Curry powder
* Ginger
* Paprika (both sweet and smoked)

Dried Herbs

I recommend keeping the following dried herbs on hand for a wide range of soups:

* **Basil** is widely used in Mediterranean countries, where it flavors everything from pasta sauces to pesto, and in Southeast Asia, where it's often stir-fried with other ingredients.

* **Bay leaves** are a staple of Mediterranean cuisines, lending a woodsy flavor to sauces, stews, and grilled meats. It's best to add whole leaves, then remove them before serving the dish.

* **Oregano** has a slightly sweet, pungent flavor that works especially well in vegetable soups and tomato-based soups. Because of its pungency, it requires caution in its use.

❀ **Rosemary** is a pungent herb with needle-like leaves. The Italians are particularly fond of it, using it to flavor meats and tomato sauces, but it is delicious with bean, vegetable, and chicken soups, too.

❀ **Rubbed sage** has a strong, woodsy aroma and is often combined with other strong herbs to flavor meat and poultry soups. It is also wonderful in combination with sweet potatoes and butternut squash. Use it sparingly; a little goes a long way.

❀ **Tarragon** is an aromatic, anise-like herb that is often found in delicately flavored French dishes. Use it sparingly; a little goes a long way.

❀ **Thyme** is a member of the mint family and has a pungent minty, light-lemon aroma that works beautifully in a wide range of soups.

Salt

Unless otherwise specified, I tested all of the recipes in this collection with ordinary table salt. Salt connoisseurs often prefer to use kosher salt, which is all natural and additive free; you are welcome to substitute it (the fine kosher salt, not the coarse) for the table salt.

Jarred Thai Curry Paste

Available in small jars, Thai curry paste is typically a blend of Thai chilies, garlic, lemon grass, galangal, ginger, and kaffir lime. It is a fast and delicious method for adding Southeast Asian flavor to soup in a single step. Panang and yellow curry pastes are typically the most mild. Red curry paste is medium hot, and green curry paste is the hottest.

Whole Peppercorns

Freshly cracked, whole fresh black peppercorns add great depth of flavor to nearly any soup. Once you begin using them for seasoning in soups and other dishes, you will never want to go back to the flavorless, preground varieties.

Pasta

Stock your pantry shelves with an assortment of pasta shapes for quick, hearty, healthy soups in no time. Use smaller shapes in thinner soups and larger shapes in thicker soups. And if you don't mind spending a little bit more, opt for multigrain pasta—it's a delicious way to incorporate whole grains into your diet with almost no effort. Here are my suggestions for types to keep on hand:

❀ Big, medium, and small shapes of pasta
❀ Couscous (regular and/or whole wheat)
❀ Israeli couscous

Grains

Given that whole grains are inexpensive, are a readily available source of protein, and have more carbohydrates than any other food, it's no wonder they're a staple throughout the world. I love adding them to soups for both heft and health. Plus, when cooked in soup they add a distinct nutty flavor and chewy texture that is both delicious and filling. I recommend keeping the following varieties on hand:

❀ **Rice** - Dozens of rice varieties exist, from all over the world, but rice is generally described as being long, medium, or short grained. Try to keep all three varieties on hand, but if you choose just one, opt for a medium grain rice for its versatility. Brown rice is by far the healthiest, but takes a while to cook. But a quick solution exists: fast-cooking brown rice. Available in pouches (e.g., Success® brand), it cooks in a fraction of the time required to cook regular brown rice.

❀ **Pearl barley** - Barley is an ancient grain that has long been a favorite in soups. It has a mild sweetness and, when cooked properly, a chewy but tender texture. Pearl barley is barley that has had the bran removed and has been steamed and polished.

❀ **Kamut** - Considered by some to be the great-great-grandfather of grains, kamut is a variety of high-protein wheat that has never been hybridized. The kernels are two to three times the size of most wheat. Not only does this grain have a deliciously nutty flavor, but it also has an impressive nutritional profile.

❀ **Farro** - An ancient variety of wheat cultivated in Italy that has recently caught the attention of cooks in the United States, farro has a nutty flavor and a firm, chewy texture that resembles barley more than wheat.

❀ **Quinoa** - Classified as a whole grain, but technically a seed, quinoa was a staple of the ancient Incas and is still an important food in South American cuisine. It contains more protein than any other grain and is also considered a "complete protein" because it contains all eight essential amino acids. Tiny in shape, quinoa cooks like rice (taking half the time of regular rice) and expands to four times its original volume. Its flavor is delicate and is often compared to couscous.

Dried Legumes

❀ **Split peas** (both green and yellow) - A variety of yellow and green peas are grown specifically for drying. These peas are dried and split along a natural seam (hence, *split peas*). Split peas are very inexpensive and loaded with good nutrition, including a significant amount of protein. They are available packaged in supermarkets and in bulk in health-food stores. Unlike dried beans, they do not require presoaking.

❀ **Lentils** (brown, French green, and red) are a boon to home cooks everywhere.

They are inexpensive, don't need soaking, cook in about 30 to 45 minutes, and are super healthy (soybeans are the only legume with more protein). Lentils also have a terrific flavor that's great in a range of soups, from earthy to slightly sweet. They come in a variety of sizes and colors: Common brown lentils and French green lentils can be found in supermarkets, and you can find the others (e.g., red and black lentils) in the international foods section, international grocery stores, and online.

Shelf-stable Tofu

Vacuum-sealed tofu, also called Japanese style or kinugoshi, is sold in aseptic boxes and is available in soft, firm, and extra-firm textures. It keeps for many months in the pantry and, diced into cubes or cut into strips, is a perfect way to add protein to a wide range of soups.

You can also follow one of my favorite tricks for upping the protein in puréed vegetable soups: add half a block of cubed tofu to the soup before puréeing. It won't impart a flavor, but will add great nutrition and some extra body to the soup.

Refrigerated Goods

Butter: When it comes to flavor, nothing compares to real butter. But because it is high in saturated fat, it is used in small quantities throughout this collection. All of the recipes were tested with unsalted butter unless otherwise stated.

Fresh butter should have a delicate cream flavor and pale yellow color. Butter quickly picks up off-flavors during storage and when exposed to oxygen; once the carton is opened, place it in a zipper-top plastic food bag or airtight container. Store it away from foods with strong odors, especially items such as onions or garlic.

Milk: Both low-fat and nonfat milk are used throughout this collection in a wide range of recipes. Be sure to note when low-fat milk is used—the extra fat is needed in that recipe, so nonfat milk should not be substituted. Similarly, do not substitute fresh low-fat or nonfat milk for canned evaporated fat-free milk; the latter has a richness similar to cream that fresh milk does not.

Low-Fat Buttermilk: Commercially prepared buttermilk is made by culturing skim or low-fat milk with bacteria. It has a distinctive tang that, when added to soups, both brightens and melds the flavors.

Nonfat and Low-fat Yogurt: Yogurt is acidic, and, like buttermilk, it brightens the flavor of a wide range of soups. It can be mixed straight into soups or spooned on top. It makes an excellent substitution for sour cream in a wide range of recipes.

Fresh Vegetables: When you're buying fresh vegetables for healthy cooking and eating, it pays to know which ones last and which ones will spoil quickly. More delicate vegetables, such as asparagus, bell peppers, corn, cucumbers, mushrooms, okra, yellow squash, and zucchini should be used close to the day of purchase. But the following are excellent choices for keeping on hand when the soup-making urge strikes:

* Onions
* Garlic
* Carrots
* Celery
* Potatoes (yellow and russet)
* Sweet potatoes
* Butternut squash
* Acorn squash
* Cabbage

Fresh Herbs

Fresh herbs add an aromatic backbone to fast, healthy soups. Added directly to ready-made broth, they willingly surrender their flavors and aromas in minutes. Or add them as a final flourish for a bright note of fresh flavor, as well as color. Keep the following on hand year-round; they are readily available, inexpensive, and keep well in the produce bin of the refrigerator:

* Flat-leaf (Italian) parsley
* Cilantro
* Green onions

Keep the following on hand in the spring and summer, when they are in season and inexpensive at farmer's markets:

* Basil
* Mint
* Thyme
* Chives

Frozen Goods

Frozen Vegetables: There's nothing wrong with using a range of frozen vegetables in your enlightened soups. In fact, if there aren't a lot of farms in your area and the markets you shop at have their produce shipped in from long distances, go frozen. Why? Frozen vegetables are frozen right after being picked to ensure that all the vitamins and minerals are preserved. If produce is shipped a long distance it can lose vitamins and minerals from exposure to heat and light. Find the brands you like best and keep them on hand as part of your quick pantry. I recommend the following:

- Winter squash purée (typically a blend of acorn and butternut squashes)
- Petite peas
- Frozen chopped greens (e.g., spinach, chard, mustard greens)
- Chopped onions
- Stir-fry bell pepper blends
- Frozen broccoli flowerets
- Shelled edamame

Frozen boneless, skinless chicken breasts: The ever-versatile chicken breast is an essential staple. If you buy them fresh, remove them from their packaging before freezing and store in small or large heavy-duty freezer bags. Alternatively, buy flash-frozen breasts; you can remove them from the package individually.

Frozen white fish fillets: I love using frozen white fish in soups; convenient and economical, the fillets absorb all of the delicious flavors of the recipe, making it hard to discern they were frozen. Available in boxes and bags, the fillets are individually sealed in vacuum pouches, meaning you can thaw a few at a time in a matter of minutes.

Frozen shrimp: Raw, deveined shrimp are nutritious, quick protein additions to soup. Buy larger quantities when they are on sale. Thaw overnight or, if you're in a hurry, in a sink of cold water, or in the microwave using the defrost function.

Equipment
Essential checklist
Great soup requires minimal equipment. Here is a short list of what you need:

- 1-cup and 2-cup liquid measuring cups (preferably clear glass or plastic)
- Dry measuring cups in graduated sizes ¼, ⅓, ½, and 1-cup measuring
- Saucepans (preferably heavy-bottomed pans)
- Kitchen/chef's knife
- Cutting boards
- Wooden spoons
- Silicone spatulas
- Electric blender (standard upright)
- Ladle
- Kitchen timer

* Upright grater/shredder
* Oven mitts or holders

Wish-list checklist
* Immersion (handheld) blender
* Food processor
* Mini hand-operated chopper (for herbs, garlic, and fresh ginger)
* Microplane grater (for grating citrus zest and cheese)

Measuring Ingredients

Measuring Dry Ingredients: When measuring a dry ingredient such as rice, pasta, couscous, or lentils, spoon it into the appropriate-size dry measuring cup or measuring spoon, heaping it up over the top. Next, slide a straight-edged utensil, such as a knife, across the top to level off the extra. Be careful not to shake or tap the cup or spoon to settle the ingredient or you will have more than you need.

Measuring Liquid Ingredients: Use a clear plastic or glass measuring cup or container with lines up the sides to measure liquid ingredients. Set the container on the counter and pour the liquid to the appropriate mark. Lower your head to read the measurement at eye level.

Measuring Butter: Butter is typically packaged in stick form with markings on the wrapper indicating tablespoon and cup measurements. Use a sharp knife to cut off the amount needed for a recipe.

¼ cup = ½ stick = 4 tablespoons = 2 ounces
½ cup = 1 stick = ¼ pound = 4 ounces
1 cup = 2 sticks = ½ pound = 8 ounces
2 cups = 4 sticks = 1 pound = 16 ounces

Measuring Dried Spices, Dried Herbs, Salt & Pepper: Use the standard measuring spoon size specified in the recipe and be sure the spoon is dry when measuring. Fill a standard measuring spoon to the top and level with a spatula or knife. When a recipe calls for a dash of a spice or salt, use about ¹⁄₁₆ of a teaspoon. A pinch is considered to be the amount of salt that can be held between the tips of the thumb and forefinger, and is also approximately ¹⁄₁₆ of a teaspoon.

Soup Storage

Soup is one of those rare and wonderful preparations that tastes even better after a day or two in the refrigerator, or even following a month-long sojourn in the deep freezer. That being said, here are my suggestions for best storing your soup.

Refrigerator Storage

Storing soup in the refrigerator is simple. Pour the completely cooled soup into a plastic storage container with a tight-fitting lid or a heavy-duty zipper-top storage bag. That's it! Almost all of the soups in this collection can be stored this way for at least two to three days.

Freezer Storage

My favorite method for storing soups in the freezer is both inexpensive and space-saving.

1. First, pour the completely cooled soup into a heavy-duty zip-top plastic bag, leaving enough room for expansion (usually an inch or two at the top).

2. Next, lay the bag flat on a baking sheet.

3. Place in the freezer until completely frozen, then remove the baking sheet. You'll be left with an easily stackable flat bag of soup.

4. To thaw, place the bag in the refrigerator for 10 to 12 hours, or cut off the bag, place in a microwave dish, and thaw using the defrost function of the microwave.

5. Reheat by placing contents in a saucepan over low heat, adding some liquid if necessary.

Note: You can follow the same method for smaller portions, too: simply use heavy-duty, sandwich-size zip-top plastic bags.

You can certainly use plastic storage containers, too. Just be sure to cool the soup completely before placing in the container and to leave some space at the top (an inch or two) before locking the lid into place (allowing for expansion when frozen).

If the soup calls for garnishes or toppings, leave them off for freezing. Write a note on the bag or container stating the intended garnish so that, when it's time to defrost, you won't have to look up the recipe.

Nutritional Analysis

A nutritional analysis follows every recipe in this book and gives the nutritional content of an individual serving. A few recipes give you a choice of ingredients, for example, "green onions or chives." The nutritional analysis is always based on the first choice. When the recipe calls for "salt to taste," the salt has not been factored into the analysis.

1. PURÉED VEGETABLE *Soups*

Classic Tomato Soup, Cream of Broccoli Soup, Leek and Potato Soup, Spring Spinach Soup with Fresh Mint Cream, Butternut Squash Soup with Sage & Thyme, Cream of Mushroom Soup, Zucchini & Spinach Soup with Lemon & Feta, Eggplant & Roasted Red Bell Pepper Soup, Winter Vegetable Bisque with Sherry & Thyme, Carrot Soup with Cilantro-Lemon Chimichurri, Petite Pea Soup with Crumbled Goat Cheese, Pumpkin Soup, Summer Corn & Basil Bisque, Roasted Red Pepper Soup, Asparagus Soup with Spring Herb Gremolata, Artichoke & Blue Cheese Bisque, Cauliflower Bisque with Apples & Indian Spices, Down Island Sweet Potato Bisque, Cold Avocado Soup with Smoky-Cilantro Cream, Chilled Honeydew-Cucumber Soup, Garden Gazpacho, and Watermelon Gazpacho

Classic Tomato Soup

This soup transports me straight back to my childhood. Tomato soup and grilled cheese sandwiches were one of my favorite weekend lunches, and when I was lucky, the combination appeared at dinner, too (usually when my mother was too pooped to cook). Canned tomatoes vary in their sweetness, so taste for that—as well as for salt and pepper—in the finished soup. You might want to add a bit more sugar to balance the acidity of the tomatoes.

1 TABLESPOON OLIVE OIL	¼ TEASPOON CAYENNE PEPPER
1½ CUPS CHOPPED ONION	¼ TEASPOON CELERY SEED
3 GARLIC CLOVES, MINCED	¼ TEASPOON DRIED OREGANO
3 14.5-OUNCE CANS WHOLE TOMATOES, UNDRAINED	⅔ CUP CANNED FAT-FREE EVAPORATED MILK (FROM A 12-OUNCE CAN)
¾ CUP WATER	2 TABLESPOONS SHERRY OR MARSALA
1 TABLESPOON SUGAR	

Heat the oil in a large saucepan set over medium heat. Add the onion, then season with salt and pepper. Cook and stir 5 minutes. Add the garlic. Cook and stir 1 minute longer.

Add the tomatoes and their juices, water, sugar, cayenne, celery seed, and oregano to the pan. Bring the soup to a boil over high heat, breaking up the tomatoes with the back of a spoon. Reduce the heat to medium and simmer 10 minutes.

Working in batches, purée the soup in a blender until smooth. Return the soup to the saucepan and stir in the milk and sherry. Season with salt and pepper to taste. Rewarm for 2 minutes to blend flavors. **Makes 6 servings.**

NUTRITION PER SERVING:
CALORIES 108; FAT 2.3G (SAT 0.7G, MONO 1.2G, POLY 0.4G); PROTEIN 5.2G;
CHOLESTEROL 2.0MG; SODIUM 397MG; CARBOHYDRATE 16.9G.

30 MINUTES

Cream of Broccoli Soup

Rich in calcium and antioxidants, but low in fat and calories, this gorgeous green soup is elegant enough for company but also just right for an easy weeknight supper.

---

1 TABLESPOON UNSALTED BUTTER

1½ CUPS CHOPPED ONION

4 CLOVES GARLIC, MINCED OR PRESSED

6 CUPS SMALL BROCCOLI FLORETS

4 CUPS LOW-SODIUM CHICKEN OR VEGETABLE BROTH

2 CUPS PACKED PREWASHED SPINACH

1 TEASPOON FRESHLY GRATED LEMON ZEST

¼ TEASPOON GROUND NUTMEG

1 12-OUNCE CAN FAT-FREE EVAPORATED MILK (OR 1½ CUPS LOW-FAT BUTTERMILK)

Melt the butter in a large saucepan set over medium heat. Add the onion and garlic, then season with salt and pepper. Cook until onion is tender, but not browned, about 10 minutes.

Add the broccoli and broth. Bring to a boil. Cook, uncovered, until the broccoli is very tender, about 8 minutes. Stir in the spinach, lemon zest, and nutmeg.

Working in batches, purée the soup in a blender until smooth. Return the soup to the saucepan and reheat gently. Stir in the evaporated milk or buttermilk. Season with salt and pepper to taste. **Makes 6 servings.**

Camilla's Note: You can substitute frozen baby broccoli florets (these are vastly superior to regular frozen broccoli) for the fresh broccoli. There is no need to defrost it. Simply add the frozen broccoli to the pan and increase cooking time by 2 minutes.

NUTRITION PER SERVING:
CALORIES 91; FAT 3.1G (SAT 1.8G, MONO 0.8G, POLY 0.2G);
PROTEIN 6.2G; CHOLESTEROL 10MG; SODIUM 418MG; CARBOHYDRATE 10.8G.

30 MINUTES

Leek and Potato Soup

You may never go back to plain old potatoes once you try this silken soup—one spoonful and you'll understand why it's a French classic. Puréeing the potatoes and leeks provides ample creaminess—I promise that you won't miss the cream or lack of extra butter.

1   TABLESPOON UNSALTED BUTTER

4   LARGE LEEKS, WHITE AND TENDER GREEN
    PARTS ONLY, WELL RINSED AND THINLY
    SLICED

2   MEDIUM RUSSET POTATOES (ABOUT ½
    POUND), PEELED AND CUT INTO 2-INCH
    CHUNKS

5   CUPS LOW-SODIUM CHICKEN OR
    VEGETABLE BROTH

1   CUP CANNED FAT-FREE EVAPORATED MILK
    (FROM A 12-OUNCE CAN)

⅛   TEASPOON GROUND NUTMEG

2   TABLESPOONS SNIPPED CHIVES

Melt the butter in a medium saucepan set over medium heat. Add the leeks, reduce heat to low, and cook, stirring occasionally, until the leeks are softened, about 8 minutes. Add the potatoes and broth, and bring to a boil. Cover partially and simmer over low heat until the potatoes are tender, about 15 minutes.

Working in batches, purée the soup in a blender until smooth. Return the soup to the saucepan, whisk in the evaporated milk and nutmeg, and reheat gently. Season with salt and pepper to taste. Serve sprinkled with chives. **Makes 6 servings.**

NUTRITION PER SERVING:
CALORIES 169; FAT 2.6G (SAT 1.4G, MONO 0.7G, POLY 0.3G);
PROTEIN 3.5G; CHOLESTEROL 6MG; SODIUM 431MG; CARBOHYDRATE 34.1G.

45 MINUTES

Spring Spinach Soup

WITH FRESH MINT CREAM

The delicate yet assertive taste of fresh mint is the perfect counterpoint to the fresh yet earthy flavor of spinach. The petite peas lend extra creaminess, color, and a subtle touch of sweetness.

1	TABLESPOON UNSALTED BUTTER	3	CUPS LOW-SODIUM CHICKEN OR VEGETABLE BROTH
1½	CUPS CHOPPED ONION	¾	CUP 2% LOW-FAT MILK, DIVIDED USE
2	CLOVES GARLIC, MINCED	¼	CUP FINELY CHOPPED FRESH MINT LEAVES
2	10-OUNCE BAGS PREWASHED SPINACH	½	CUP REDUCED-FAT SOUR CREAM
1	CUP FROZEN PETITE PEAS, UNTHAWED		

Melt the butter in a large saucepan set over medium heat. Add the onion and garlic, then season with salt and pepper. Cook until onion is tender, but not browned, about 10 minutes.

Add the spinach and sauté 4 to 5 minutes or until wilted. Add the peas and broth and bring to a boil. Lower heat and simmer, uncovered, for 10 minutes. Remove the soup from heat.

Working in batches, purée the soup in a blender until smooth. Return the soup to the saucepan and reheat gently. Stir in ½ cup of the milk. Season with salt and pepper to taste. Keep warm.

In a small bowl whisk the mint, sour cream, and remaining ¼ cup milk until blended.

Serve soup with a dollop or swirl of the mint cream. **Makes 6 servings.**

NUTRITION PER SERVING:
CALORIES 165; FAT 3.5G (SAT 0.6G, MONO 1.3G, POLY 0.3G);
PROTEIN 5.7G; CHOLESTEROL 0.0MG; SODIUM 787MG; CARBOHYDRATE 32.4G.

30 MINUTES

Butternut Squash Soup

WITH SAGE & THYME

It's hard to believe there's no cream—and only a small amount of butter—in this soup; it's so velvety. The buttermilk adds richness and complexity (without the high fat and calorie content of heavy cream) and also brightens the sweetness of the squash.

2 TABLESPOONS UNSALTED BUTTER	8 CUPS PEELED BUTTERNUT SQUASH, CUT
1¼ CUPS CHOPPED ONION (ABOUT 1 MEDIUM	INTO 1-INCH PIECES (ABOUT 3 POUNDS)
ONION)	1¼ TEASPOONS DRIED RUBBED SAGE
4 LARGE CLOVES GARLIC, MINCED	1 TEASPOON DRIED THYME LEAVES,
5⅓ CUPS LOW-SODIUM CHICKEN OR	CRUMBLED
VEGETABLE BROTH	⅓ CUP LOW-FAT BUTTERMILK
	1 TABLESPOON LIGHT BROWN SUGAR

Melt the butter in a large saucepan set over medium heat. Add the onion and garlic, then season with salt and pepper. Cook until onion is tender, but not browned, about 10 minutes. Add the broth, squash, sage, and thyme and bring to a boil. Reduce heat, cover, and simmer until squash is very tender, about 20 minutes.

Working in batches, purée the soup in a blender until smooth. Return the soup to the saucepan and reheat gently. Stir in the buttermilk and brown sugar and bring to a simmer (do not boil). Season with salt and pepper to taste. **Makes 8 servings.**

Camilla's Note: You can substitute four 12-ounce packages frozen (thawed) winter squash purée for the 8 cups butternut squash. Reduce cooking time from 20 minutes to 5 minutes. Total time to prepare soup is reduced to 25 minutes.

NUTRITION PER SERVING:
CALORIES 167; FAT 3.5G (SAT 0.5G, MONO 2.2G, POLY 0.6G);
PROTEIN 4.1G; CHOLESTEROL 0MG; SODIUM 351MG; CARBOHYDRATE 33.5G.

45 MINUTES

(or 25 minutes with quick option; see note above)

Cream of Mushroom Soup

I love mushrooms. So to me, this soup, with its earthy flavor punctuated by hints of thyme and nutmeg, and smooth, velvety texture, is close to perfection.

1 TABLESPOON OLIVE OIL	3½ CUPS LOW-SODIUM CHICKEN OR
¾ CUP FINELY CHOPPED ONION	VEGETABLE BROTH, DIVIDED USE
2 12-OUNCE PACKAGES SLICED BUTTON	½ CUP 2% LOW-FAT MILK
MUSHROOMS	¼ TEASPOON GROUND NUTMEG
1 TEASPOON DRIED THYME LEAVES	½ CUP REDUCED-FAT SOUR CREAM, DIVIDED
⅓ CUP CREAM SHERRY	USE
3 TABLESPOONS ALL-PURPOSE FLOUR	OPTIONAL: FRESH CHOPPED PARSLEY LEAVES

Heat the oil in a large saucepan set over medium heat. Add the onion and cook until tender, about 2 to 3 minutes. Add the mushrooms and thyme, then season with salt and pepper. Cook until all of the liquid rendered from the mushrooms evaporates. Add the sherry and cook until the alcohol evaporates.

Stir in the flour and cook for 2 minutes. Add 3 cups of the broth, bring to a simmer, and cook for 15 minutes.

Working in batches, purée the soup in a blender until smooth. Return the soup to the saucepan and reheat gently. Whisk in the milk and add some of the remaining ½ cup broth to achieve desired consistency. Season with salt and pepper to taste.

Lower heat and whisk in the nutmeg and ¼ cup of the sour cream. Keep soup warm but do not simmer or boil. Serve the soup with a dollop of the remaining sour cream and, if desired, chopped parsley. **Makes 6 servings.**

NUTRITION PER SERVING:
CALORIES 114; FAT 3.1G (SAT 1.8G, MONO 0.9G, POLY 0.1G);
PROTEIN 7.1G; CHOLESTEROL 11MG; SODIUM 341MG; CARBOHYDRATE 13.3G.

30 MINUTES

Zucchini & Spinach Soup

WITH LEMON & FETA

A quick spin in the blender plus a topping of piquant feta cheese creates a noteworthy, seasonal soup.

1	TABLESPOON OLIVE OIL	1	TABLESPOON FRESH LEMON JUICE
2	CUPS CHOPPED ONION	2	TEASPOONS GRATED LEMON ZEST
2	CLOVES GARLIC, MINCED	½	TEASPOON GROUND CORIANDER
1½	POUNDS ZUCCHINI, TRIMMED, CUT INTO ½-INCH-THICK ROUNDS	1	6-OUNCE BAG PREWASHED BABY SPINACH
1	12-OUNCE RUSSET POTATO, PEELED AND THINLY SLICED	1½	CUPS CILANTRO LEAVES, COARSELY CHOPPED
4	CUPS LOW-SODIUM CHICKEN OR VEGETABLE BROTH	2	OUNCES FETA CHEESE, CRUMBLED

Heat the oil in a large saucepan set over medium heat. Add the onion and garlic, then season with salt and pepper. Cook until the onion is tender, but not browned, about 10 minutes.

Add the zucchini and potato; stir to coat. Add the broth and bring to a boil. Reduce heat to medium low, cover, and simmer until the potato is soft, about 15 minutes. Stir in the lemon juice, lemon zest, and coriander.

Working in batches, purée the soup in a blender until smooth, adding some spinach and cilantro to each batch. Return the soup to the saucepan and reheat gently. Season with salt and pepper to taste. Serve sprinkled with the feta. **Makes 8 servings.**

NUTRITION PER SERVING:
CALORIES 125; FAT 3.5G (SAT 0.5G, MONO 1.7G, POLY 1.0G);
PROTEIN 5.5G; CHOLESTEROL 0MG; SODIUM 558MG; CARBOHYDRATE 19.2G.

45 MINUTES

Eggplant & Roasted Red Bell Pepper Soup

The labor is minimal, but it pays tenfold (or more) in flavor. The luscious (but healthy) result is great paired with toasted pita bread.

1   EGGPLANT (ABOUT 1¼ POUNDS), PEELED, CUT INTO 1-INCH CUBES

2   TABLESPOONS OLIVE OIL, DIVIDED USE

2   CUPS CHOPPED ONION

3   LARGE GARLIC CLOVES, MINCED

1   12-OUNCE JAR ROASTED RED BELL PEPPERS, DRAINED, COARSELY CHOPPED

4¼ CUPS LOW-SODIUM CHICKEN OR VEGETABLE BROTH

3   TABLESPOONS TOMATO PASTE

1   TEASPOON DRIED OREGANO LEAVES

1   TEASPOON DRIED THYME LEAVES

2   TEASPOONS FRESH LEMON JUICE

OPTIONAL: FRESH BASIL, SLICED INTO RIBBONS

PARMESAN CHEESE SHAVINGS

Place the eggplant in a large microwave-safe dish or bowl and toss with 1 tablespoon of the oil. Season with salt and pepper. Microwave on high for 5 minutes.

Heat the remaining tablespoon oil in large pot set over medium-high heat. Add the onion and garlic, then season with salt and pepper. Cook and stir 5 minutes. Stir in the eggplant, peppers, broth, and tomato paste. Bring to a boil. Reduce heat to medium and simmer uncovered 20 minutes. Stir in the oregano, thyme, and lemon juice.

Working in batches, purée the soup in a blender until smooth. Return the soup to the saucepan and reheat gently. Season with salt and pepper to taste. Serve sprinkled with basil and Parmesan shavings. **Makes 6 servings.**

NUTRITION PER SERVING:
CALORIES 214; FAT 6.5G (SAT 0.8G, MONO 3.4G, POLY 0.6G);
PROTEIN 7.5G; CHOLESTEROL 1MG; SODIUM 323MG; CARBOHYDRATE 37.1G.

45 MINUTES

Winter Vegetable Bisque

WITH SHERRY & THYME

This soup was inspired by stoemp, *a Belgian dish of mashed potatoes with vegetables. As good as it is the day it's made, it is even better the day after for lunch.*

1 TABLESPOON UNSALTED BUTTER	1 TEASPOON DRIED THYME LEAVES
2½ CUPS CHOPPED ONION	¼ TEASPOON GROUND NUTMEG
2 CUPS PEELED AND SLICED CARROTS	6 TABLESPOONS CHOPPED FRESH FLAT-LEAF
1 CUP PEELED AND SLICED PARSNIPS	PARSLEY LEAVES, DIVIDED USE
3½ CUPS LOW-SODIUM CHICKEN OR	1 12-OUNCE CAN EVAPORATED FAT-FREE
VEGETABLE BROTH, PLUS ADDITIONAL	MILK
2½ CUPS CUBED YUKON GOLD POTATOES	3 TABLESPOONS SHERRY

Melt the butter in a large saucepan set over medium heat. Add the onion. Season with salt and pepper. Cook and stir 5 minutes. Add the carrots and parsnips. Cook and stir 5 minutes.

Add the broth, potatoes, thyme, nutmeg, and 4 tablespoons of the parsley. Cover and simmer 25 minutes, until the potatoes are tender, stirring occasionally.

Working in batches, purée the soup in a blender until smooth. Return the soup to the saucepan and reheat gently. Stir in the evaporated milk and sherry. Season with salt and pepper to taste.

Bring soup to a simmer, thinning with additional broth, if desired. Ladle into bowls and serve sprinkled with the remaining parsley. **Makes 8 servings.**

NUTRITION PER SERVING:
CALORIES 169; FAT 2.2G (SAT 1.2G, MONO 0.6G, POLY 0.1G);
PROTEIN 5.5G; CHOLESTEROL 8MG; SODIUM 496MG; CARBOHYDRATE 32.9G.

60 MINUTES

Carrot Soup

WITH CILANTRO-LEMON CHIMICHURRI

This soup is perfectly outfitted for spring with a cheery blend of carrots and spring onions, plus a sweet-tart lemon chimichurri for zing.

5 LARGE CARROTS (ABOUT 1½ POUNDS), PEELED AND CUT INTO ½-INCH PIECES	1 CUP 2% LOW-FAT MILK
3½ CUPS LOW-SODIUM CHICKEN OR VEGETABLE BROTH	1½ CUPS LOOSELY PACKED FRESH CILANTRO LEAVES
1½ CUPS CHOPPED ONION	½ CUP SLICED GREEN ONIONS
2 LARGE BAY LEAVES	2 TABLESPOONS FRESH LEMON JUICE
¼ TEASPOON GROUND ALLSPICE	2 TABLESPOONS WATER
¾ CUP DRAINED CANNED WHITE BEANS (FROM A 15-OUNCE CAN)	1 TABLESPOON HONEY
	1 GARLIC CLOVE, PEELED
	¼ TEASPOON CAYENNE PEPPER

Place the carrots, broth, onion, bay leaves, and allspice in a medium saucepan set over high heat. Bring to a boil. Reduce heat to low, cover, and simmer until carrots are tender, about 15 minutes. Remove the bay leaves.

Working in batches, purée soup in a blender until smooth, adding some of the white beans with each batch. Return soup to saucepan and whisk in the milk. Stir over low heat until heated through. Season with salt and pepper to taste.

To make the chimichurri sauce, process the cilantro, green onions, lemon juice, water, honey, garlic, and cayenne in a blender or food processor until smooth. Season with salt and pepper to taste. Serve soup drizzled with the chimichurri. **Makes 6 servings.**

NUTRITION PER SERVING:
CALORIES 153; FAT 3.7G (SAT 1.3G, MONO 1.8G, POLY 0.3G);
PROTEIN 4.8G; CHOLESTEROL 8MG; SODIUM 461MG; CARBOHYDRATE 26.1G.

30 MINUTES

Petite Pea Soup

WITH CRUMBLED GOAT CHEESE

Regardless of your feelings about frozen peas, you will love this soup. Its short list of humble ingredients belies its elegance and depth of flavor.

1 TABLESPOON OLIVE OIL

1 CUP CHOPPED ONION (ABOUT 1 SMALL ONION)

1 SMALL BOILING POTATO (ABOUT 4 OR 5 OUNCES), PEELED AND CUT INTO ½-INCH PIECES

3½ CUPS LOW-SODIUM CHICKEN OR VEGETABLE BROTH

1 1-POUND BAG FROZEN PETITE PEAS

1 TABLESPOON CHOPPED FRESH TARRAGON LEAVES (OR 1½ TEASPOONS DRIED, CRUMBLED)

2 OUNCES SOFT FRESH GOAT CHEESE, CRUMBLED

Heat the oil in a large saucepan set over medium heat. Add the onion. Season with salt and pepper. Cook and stir 3 minutes.

Add the potato and broth. Bring to a boil. Reduce heat to low and simmer, covered, until the potato is tender, about 15 minutes. Add the peas and tarragon, and simmer, uncovered, 2 minutes.

Working in batches, purée the soup in a blender until smooth. Return the soup to the saucepan and reheat gently. Season with salt and pepper to taste. Serve soup sprinkled with the goat cheese. **Makes 6 servings.**

NUTRITION PER SERVING:
CALORIES 161; FAT 5.3G (SAT 1.4G, MONO 2.9G, POLY 0.7G);
PROTEIN 8.6G; CHOLESTEROL 3.3MG; SODIUM 311MG; CARBOHYDRATE 20.8G.

30 MINUTES

Pumpkin Soup

The flavor of this pumpkin soup is so pleasing—familiar spices and a touch of orange—and the texture so voluptuous that you'll wonder how such modest ingredients could conspire to create something so indulgent. If you need any more reasons to try it, how about low cost, low calories, low fat, and 30 minutes from stove to table.

1 TABLESPOON OLIVE OIL	2½ CUPS LOW-SODIUM CHICKEN OR
1 CUP CHOPPED ONION	VEGETABLE BROTH
2 LARGE CLOVES GARLIC, MINCED	½ CUP ORANGE JUICE
½ TEASPOON GROUND ALLSPICE	1 15-OUNCE CAN SOLID PACK PUMPKIN
½ TEASPOON GROUND GINGER	1 12-OUNCE CAN FAT-FREE EVAPORATED MILK

Heat the oil in a medium saucepan set over medium heat. Add the onion, garlic, allspice, and ginger, then season with salt and pepper. Cook and stir 5 minutes.

Whisk in the broth, orange juice, and pumpkin. Bring to a boil. Reduce heat to low and simmer 10 minutes, stirring occasionally.

Working in batches, purée the soup in a blender until smooth. Return the soup to the saucepan, whisk in the evaporated milk, and reheat gently. Season with salt and pepper to taste. Serve warm. **Makes 6 servings.**

NUTRITION PER SERVING:
CALORIES 122; FAT 3.1G (SAT 0.8G, MONO 1.2G, POLY 0.7G);
PROTEIN 5.5G; CHOLESTEROL 1MG; SODIUM 228MG; CARBOHYDRATE 19.9G.

30 MINUTES

Summer Corn & Basil Bisque

This soup is particularly delicious when made with sweet white corn, but yellow corn (including frozen) still produces delectable results. If you use fresh corn, remove the kernels from the cobs by holding each ear of corn upright on a flat surface and running a chef's knife along the cob and cutting downward, as close to the cob as possible.

4 TEASPOONS UNSALTED BUTTER, DIVIDED USE	3 CUPS LOW-SODIUM CHICKEN OR VEGETABLE BROTH
1 CUP CHOPPED ONION	1 CUP LOOSELY PACKED BASIL LEAVES, DIVIDED USE
⅓ CUP DICED CARROT	⅔ CUP CANNED FAT-FREE EVAPORATED MILK (FROM A 12-OUNCE CAN)
⅓ CUP DICED CELERY	
4 CUPS FRESH (OR FROZEN, THAWED) CORN KERNELS	1 MEDIUM RED BELL PEPPER, SEEDED AND CHOPPED
¼ TEASPOON CAYENNE PEPPER	

Melt 2 teaspoons of the butter in a medium saucepan set over medium heat. Add the onion, carrot, and celery, then season with salt and pepper. Cook and stir 3 minutes. Add the corn and cayenne and cook 2 minutes.

Add the broth and bring to boil. Reduce heat to medium low and simmer 15 minutes. Stir in half of the basil.

Working in batches, purée the soup in a blender until smooth. Return the soup to the saucepan, whisk in the evaporated milk, and reheat gently. Season with salt and pepper to taste.

Slice remaining basil into slivers. Melt the remaining 2 teaspoons butter in a heavy, large skillet over medium-high heat. Add the bell pepper and sauté until almost tender, about 5 minutes. Bring the soup to a simmer. Ladle into bowls and top with the bell pepper and basil. **Makes 6 servings.**

NUTRITION PER SERVING:
CALORIES 147; FAT 3.2G (SAT 1.2G, MONO 1.2G, POLY 0.5G);
PROTEIN 7.6G; CHOLESTEROL 12MG; SODIUM 549 MG; CARBOHYDRATE 25G.

30 MINUTES

Roasted Red Pepper Soup

At once lush and light, this brilliant-red soup is as delicious cold as it is warm.

8 MEDIUM RED BELL PEPPERS, SEEDED AND SLICED IN HALVES LENGTHWISE	4 CUPS FAT-FREE, LESS-SODIUM CHICKEN BROTH
2 TEASPOONS OLIVE OIL	2 TABLESPOONS WHITE WINE VINEGAR
2 CUPS CHOPPED ONION	½ TEASPOON HOT PEPPER SAUCE
3 CLOVES GARLIC, MINCED	2 TABLESPOONS CHOPPED FRESH CHIVES
1 BAY LEAF	

Preheat the broiler. Place the pepper halves, skin sides up, on a foil-lined baking sheet; flatten with your hand. Broil for 15 minutes or until blackened. Place in a zip-top plastic bag; seal. Let the peppers cool for 15 minutes, then peel and chop.

Heat the oil in a large saucepan set over medium-high heat. Add the onion. Season with salt and pepper. Cook and stir 10 minutes. Add the garlic. Cook and stir 1 minute.

Add the bell peppers, bay leaf, broth, vinegar, and hot pepper sauce. Bring to a boil. Cover, reduce heat, and simmer 15 minutes. Remove and discard the bay leaf.

Working in batches, purée the soup in a blender until smooth. Return the soup to the saucepan. Season with salt and pepper to taste. Serve sprinkled with the chives. **Makes 6 servings.**

NUTRITION PER SERVING:
CALORIES 99; FAT 2.4G (SAT 0.4G, MONO 1.2G, POLY 0.5G);
PROTEIN 3.7G; CHOLESTEROL 0.0MG; SODIUM 465MG; CARBOHYDRATE 16.7G.

60 MINUTES

Asparagus Soup

WITH SPRING HERB GREMOLATA

Gremolata is a quickly assembled garnish made of minced parsley, lemon zest, and garlic. It is most familiar sprinkled over osso buco, but it adds an equally sprightly finish to lighter fare, such as this elegant asparagus soup.

2 TEASPOONS OLIVE OIL	1 TABLESPOON FRESH LEMON JUICE
1 CUP CHOPPED ONION	2 TABLESPOONS MINCED FRESH ITALIAN
1½ POUNDS ASPARAGUS, ENDS TRIMMED,	PARSLEY LEAVES
SPEARS COARSELY CHOPPED	4 TEASPOONS FINELY GRATED LEMON ZEST
4 CUPS LOW-SODIUM CHICKEN OR	1 TABLESPOON MINCED FRESH TARRAGON
VEGETABLE BROTH	LEAVES
3 CUPS PACKED PREWASHED SPINACH	1 SMALL GARLIC CLOVE, MINCED

Heat the oil in a large saucepan set over medium heat. Add the onion, then cook and stir 5 minutes. Add the asparagus and broth and bring to a boil. Reduce heat to medium, cover, and simmer until the asparagus is tender, about 8 minutes.

Add the spinach to the pan. Cover and simmer 1 to 2 minutes, until the spinach is wilted.

Working in batches, purée the soup in a blender until smooth. Return the soup to the saucepan and stir in the lemon juice. Season with salt and pepper to taste.

To make the gremolata, in a small bowl mix the parsley, lemon zest, tarragon, and garlic. Serve the soup sprinkled with the gremolata. **Makes 6 servings.**

NUTRITION PER SERVING:
CALORIES 49; FAT 1.3G (SAT 0.2G, MONO 0.6G, POLY 0.4G);
PROTEIN 2.9G; CHOLESTEROL 0.0MG; SODIUM 113MG; CARBOHYDRATE 6.9G.

30 MINUTES

Artichoke & Blue Cheese Bisque

Blue cheese adds a pungent note to this silky, warming soup. You'll be hard-pressed to tell it's a light recipe.

1 TABLESPOON UNSALTED BUTTER	½ TEASPOON DRIED THYME
1 CUP CHOPPED ONION	½ CUP CANNED FAT-FREE EVAPORATED MILK
⅓ CUP DRY WHITE WINE	(FROM A 12-OUNCE CAN)
2 8-OUNCE PACKAGES FROZEN (THAWED)	½ CRUMBLED BLUE CHEESE (ABOUT 2
ARTICHOKE HEARTS, THAWED	OUNCES)
1 SMALL RUSSET POTATO, PEELED AND	3 TABLESPOONS CHOPPED FRESH CHIVES
DICED	SPRINKLE OF PAPRIKA
3 CUPS LOW-SODIUM CHICKEN OR	
VEGETABLE BROTH	

Melt the butter in a large saucepan set over medium heat. Add the onion. Season with salt and pepper. Cook and stir 5 minutes. Add the wine and simmer until almost all the liquid evaporates, about 4 minutes.

Add the artichokes, potato, broth, and thyme. Bring to a boil, then reduce heat to low and simmer 10 minutes or until the potatoes are very tender and the artichoke hearts begin to fall apart. Remove the soup from heat.

Working in batches, purée the soup in a blender until smooth. Return the soup to the saucepan and stir in the evaporated milk and blue cheese. Simmer over medium heat, whisking constantly, until the cheese melts and the soup is smooth, about 2 minutes. Season with salt and pepper to taste. Serve sprinkled with the chives and a dash of paprika. **Makes 6 servings.**

NUTRITION PER SERVING:
CALORIES 153; FAT 8.4 G (SAT 4.1G, MONO 2.1G, POLY 1.3G);
PROTEIN 6.2G; CHOLESTEROL 71MG; SODIUM 129MG; CARBOHYDRATE 12G.

30 MINUTES

Cauliflower Bisque

WITH APPLES & INDIAN SPICES

What's a food lover to do if she lives in a small town with no Indian restaurants? Whip out the spices and start cooking. I used cauliflower as my base for this elegant soup since it is used in a wide range of Indian dishes; it serves as a fine foil to bold flavors but also has a distinctive, nutty flavor all its own. Get ready: This soup will wow you with its sublime balance of spices, subtle sweetness, and buttery-velvet texture.

1	TABLESPOON CANOLA OIL	4	CUPS CAULIFLOWER FLOWERETS (ABOUT 1 LARGE HEAD)
1	CUP CHOPPED ONION		
2	GARLIC CLOVES, MINCED	3	CUPS LOW-SODIUM CHICKEN OR VEGETABLE BROTH
1	TABLESPOON PEELED, MINCED FRESH GINGER		
		¼	CUP CANNED FAT-FREE EVAPORATED MILK (FROM A 12-OUNCE CAN)
2	TEASPOONS CURRY POWDER		
½	TEASPOON GARAM MASALA	¼	CUP CHOPPED FRESH MINT LEAVES (OR CILANTRO)
2	LARGE GRANNY SMITH APPLES, PEELED, CORED, AND COARSELY CHOPPED		

Heat the oil in a large saucepan set over medium heat. Add the onion, then cook and stir 5 minutes. Add the garlic, ginger, curry powder, and garam masala and cook 2 minutes longer.

Add the apples, cauliflower, and broth to the pan. Increase the heat to high and bring the mixture to a boil. Reduce the heat to low and simmer, covered, 25 minutes or until the cauliflower is very tender.

Working in batches, purée the soup in a blender until smooth. Return the soup to the saucepan and stir in the evaporated milk. Season with salt and pepper to taste. Serve sprinkled with the chopped mint or cilantro. **Makes 4 servings.**

NUTRITION PER SERVING:
CALORIES 88; FAT 2.5G (SAT 0.9G, MONO 1.2G, POLY 0.3G);
PROTEIN 6.4G; CHOLESTEROL 4MG; SODIUM 223MG; CARBOHYDRATE 12.1G.

60
MINUTES

Down Island Sweet Potato Bisque

As an avowed lover of all things sweet potato, I am unabashedly beholden to this soup. It has just the right balance of sweet, savory, and spice—and you can't beat the easy preparation and light profile. A winner in every way!

4 CUPS LOW-SODIUM CHICKEN OR
VEGETABLE BROTH

2 POUNDS RED-SKINNED SWEET POTATOES
(YAMS), PEELED AND CUT INTO ½-INCH
PIECES

1 CUP CANNED LIGHT COCONUT MILK

1¼ TEASPOONS CURRY POWDER

½ TEASPOON GROUND ALLSPICE

⅓ CUP PLAIN NONFAT YOGURT

3 TABLESPOONS CHOPPED FRESH CILANTRO
LEAVES

Bring the broth to a boil in a large saucepan set over medium-high heat. Add the sweet potatoes, then reduce heat to low. Cover and simmer until the sweet potatoes are very tender, about 20 minutes.

Using a slotted spoon, transfer the sweet potatoes to a blender. Add 1 cup of the broth and process until smooth.

Return the mixture to the saucepan. Whisk in the coconut milk, curry powder, and allspice. Bring to a simmer. Season with salt and pepper to taste. Serve with dollops of the yogurt and sprinkled with the cilantro. **Makes 6 servings.**

NUTRITION PER SERVING:
CALORIES 136; FAT 0.5G (SAT 0.1G, MONO 0.1G, POLY 0.2G);
PROTEIN 5.0G; CHOLESTEROL 2.0MG; SODIUM 416MG; CARBOHYDRATE 27.2G.

45 MINUTES

Cold Avocado Soup

WITH SMOKY-CILANTRO CREAM

Although refined and gorgeous, this elegant soup is a snap to make. The unctuous richness of the avocadoes is downright delectable in soup form; it's perfectly suited to hot-summer-night dinners with little more than fresh bread in accompaniment and ripe fruit for dessert.

3 LARGE RIPE CALIFORNIA AVOCADOS (ABOUT 1½ POUNDS), PEELED, PITTED, AND HALVED	1 TEASPOON GROUND CUMIN
2 TABLESPOONS FRESH LIME JUICE, OR TO TASTE	¾ TEASPOON CHIPOTLE CHILE POWDER, DIVIDED USE
1½ CUPS LOW-SODIUM VEGETABLE BROTH	½ CUP REDUCED-FAT SOUR CREAM
1½ CUPS LOW-FAT BUTTERMILK, WELL-CHILLED	2 GARLIC CLOVES, MINCED
2½ CUPS ICE WATER, DIVIDED USE	2 CUPS PACKED FRESH CILANTRO LEAVES
	GARNISH: ADDITIONAL CILANTRO SPRIGS

Place the avocados, lime juice, and broth in a blender and purée until smooth.

Transfer to a large bowl and whisk in the buttermilk, 2 cups of the ice water, cumin, ¼ teaspoon of the chipotle chile powder, and salt and pepper to taste until smooth. Thin the soup with enough of the remaining ice water to reach the desired consistency.

Chill, covered with plastic wrap, until very cold, at least 30 minutes (but no longer than 4 hours—the soup will discolor if kept longer).

For the accompanying cream, process the sour cream, garlic, cilantro, and remaining ½ teaspoon chile powder in a blender, scraping down sides, until very smooth. Season with salt and pepper to taste. Chill, covered, until ready to use.

Serve the soup drizzled with the smoky-cilantro cream and garnished with cilantro sprigs. **Makes 6 servings.**

NUTRITION PER SERVING:
CALORIES 152; FAT 8.2G (SAT 2.2G, MONO 4.3G, POLY 1.6G);
PROTEIN 6.2G; CHOLESTEROL 32MG; SODIUM 576MG; CARBOHYDRATE 18.4G.

45 MINUTES

Chilled Honeydew–Cucumber Soup

Though pale green and delicate in flavor, honeydew packs a nutritional punch: It's a good source of vitamin B$_6$, folate, and potassium, and a very good source of vitamin C. Here it stars in an elegant soup that can be served as a first course or in shot glasses for a refreshing appetizer. Lime juice adds a bright crispness, cardamom an exotic finish.

1 MEDIUM-LARGE ENGLISH (SEEDLESS) CHILLED CUCUMBER, PEELED AND CUT INTO 1-INCH PIECES	¾ CUP PLAIN LOW-FAT YOGURT
	¼ CUP FRESH LIME JUICE
	2 TEASPOONS SUGAR
3 CUPS RIPE HONEYDEW PIECES (ABOUT 1 MEDIUM MELON), WELL CHILLED	½ TEASPOON GROUND CARDAMOM
	OPTIONAL: FRESH MINT SPRIGS FOR GARNISH
¼ CUP FRESH MINT LEAVES	

Working in batches, purée the cucumber, honeydew, and mint in a blender until smooth.

Transfer the mixture to a large bowl. Whisk in the yogurt, lime juice, sugar, and cardamom. Season with salt and pepper to taste. Chill the soup, covered, at least 30 minutes, until cold. Serve garnished with the mint sprigs, if desired. **Makes 4 servings.**

NUTRITION PER SERVING:
CALORIES 161; FAT 0.6G (SAT 0.3G, MONO 0.1G, POLY 0.1G);
PROTEIN 1.8G; CHOLESTEROL 0.0MG; SODIUM 29MG; CARBOHYDRATE 37.5G.

45 MINUTES

Garden Gazpacho

Gazpacho is a cold, summertime soup from the Andalusian region of southern Spain. It is uncooked and is typically made from a puréed mixture of fresh tomatoes, sweet bell peppers, onions, celery, cucumber, bread crumbs, garlic, olive oil, vinegar and sometimes lemon juice; variations are too numerous to count. For a smoother texture to my version, simply process the soup until very smooth, then press the mixture through a sieve over a bowl, discarding the solids.

1½ POUNDS RIPE TOMATOES, EACH CUT INTO QUARTERS	½ CUP COARSELY CHOPPED GREEN BELL PEPPER
1 CUP COARSELY CHOPPED PEELED, SEEDED CUCUMBER	3 TABLESPOONS SHERRY VINEGAR
½ CUP COARSELY CHOPPED VIDALIA OR OTHER SWEET ONION	2 TABLESPOONS OLIVE OIL
½ CUP COARSELY CHOPPED RED BELL PEPPER	½ TEASPOON SALT
	¼ TEASPOON SUGAR
	¼ TEASPOON GROUND CUMIN
	5 GARLIC CLOVES, COARSELY CHOPPED

Place all of the ingredients in the bowl of a large food processor. Process until mostly, but not entirely, smooth. Cover and chill at least 30 minutes to allow the flavors to blend. Season with salt and pepper to taste. **Makes 4 servings.**

NUTRITION PER SERVING:
CALORIES 87; FAT 5.2G (SAT 0.9G, MONO 3.6G, POLY 0.7G);
PROTEIN 1.6G; CHOLESTEROL 0MG; SODIUM 217MG; CARBOHYDRATE 14G.

45 MINUTES

Watermelon Gazpacho

Use red or yellow watermelon (or both) for this summery soup, and pair the finished product with the best store-bought jalapeno-cheddar bread you can find. It's a perfect side dish to summer grilling, too.

6 CUPS CUBED WATERMELON, SEEDS REMOVED	3 TABLESPOONS CHOPPED FRESH MINT LEAVES
1 CUP COARSELY CHOPPED PEELED, SEEDED CUCUMBER	3 TABLESPOONS FRESH LIME JUICE
½ CUP COARSELY CHOPPED RED BELL PEPPER	½ TEASPOON HOT SAUCE
⅓ CUP CHOPPED GREEN ONIONS	1 GARLIC CLOVE, MINCED
	1 CUP CRANBERRY JUICE

In a large bowl combine all of the ingredients except the cranberry juice. Working in batches, purée the soup in a blender until smooth, placing the puréed mixture into a separate large bowl. Stir in the cranberry juice. Cover and chill at least 30 minutes to allow the flavors to blend. Season with salt to taste. **Makes 4 servings.**

NUTRITION PER SERVING:
CALORIES 89; FAT 2.5G (SAT 0.5G, MONO 1.6G, POLY 0.5G);
PROTEIN 1.2G; CHOLESTEROL 0MG; SODIUM 221MG; CARBOHYDRATE 16.8G.

45 MINUTES

2. VEGETABLE

Soups

BIG-BATCH VEGETABLE **SOUP**, ROASTED VEGETABLE **MINESTRONE**, IRISH CABBAGE **SOUP**, DIJON VEGETABLE **CHOWDER**, CARAMELIZED ONION **SOUP** WITH RED WINE & GOAT CHEESE CROUTONS, WILD MUSHROOM **SOUP**, JAPANESE SOBA **SOUP** WITH MISO & VEGETABLES, TUSCAN BREAD **SOUP** (RIBOLLITA), WINTER SQUASH **SOUP** WITH CUMIN, KALE & BACON, PEASANT **SOUP** WITH BROCCOLI RABE, TOMATOES & CANNELLINI, WINTER **MINESTRONE** WITH FENNEL, CHARD & POTATOES, RUSTIC TOMATO **SOUP** WITH PASTA & PESTO, SMOKY CORN **CHOWDER**, GARLICKY SPINACH & TOMATO **SOUP** WITH CHEESE RAVIOLI, CURRIED COUSCOUS, SPINACH & ROASTED TOMATO **SOUP**, PUNJABI POTATO & CAULIFLOWER **SOUP** WITH MINTED YOGURT, SOUPE AU PISTOU, HOMINY, TOMATO, & CHILE **SOUP**, CHINESE-STYLE BOK CHOY & MUSHROOM **SOUP**, DUTCH FARMER'S CHEESE & VEGETABLE **SOUP**, GNOCCHI **SOUP** WITH ROOT VEGETABLES, LEMON & DILL, CHINESE HOT & SOUR **SOUP**, SPICY SWEET POTATO & COCONUT **SOUP**, VEGETABLE TORTELLINI **SOUP** WITH ASPARAGUS, PEAS & PARMESAN, AND GREEN CHILE **CHOWDER**

Big-Batch Vegetable Soup

In this easy and hugely versatile soup, an assortment of vegetables is transformed into a boast-worthy main dish. And because you can use either frozen or fresh vegetables, it's a soup to be made and enjoyed year-round.

1 TABLESPOON OLIVE OIL	1 28-OUNCE CAN DICED TOMATOES, UNDRAINED
2 CUPS CHOPPED ONION	¼ CUP TOMATO PASTE
1 CUP THINLY SLICED CELERY	8 CUPS MIXED FRESH VEGETABLES, SUCH AS CARROTS, CORN, GREEN BEANS, EDAMAME, PEAS, POTATOES, AND ZUCCHINI (CUT LARGER VEGETABLES INTO BITE-SIZE PIECES)
2 TEASPOONS DRIED BASIL	
1 TEASPOON DRIED OREGANO	
5½ CUPS LOW-SODIUM CHICKEN OR VEGETABLE BROTH	
3 CUPS WATER	

Heat the oil in a large saucepan set over medium heat. Add the onion, celery, basil, and oregano. Season with salt and pepper. Cook and stir 8 minutes.

Add the broth, water, tomatoes with their juices, and tomato paste. Bring the mixture to a boil, then reduce heat to a simmer and cook, uncovered, 20 minutes. Stir in the vegetables and return to a simmer. Cook, uncovered, until vegetables are tender, about 25 minutes. Season with salt and pepper to taste. **Makes 8 servings.**

Camilla's Note: To save time, you can use a mix of different frozen vegetables for the fresh vegetables.

NUTRITION PER SERVING:
CALORIES 111; FAT 2.1G (SAT 0.5G, MONO 1.3G, POLY 0.3G);
PROTEIN 4.7G; CHOLESTEROL 0.0MG; SODIUM 389MG; CARBOHYDRATE 31.1G.

60 MINUTES

Roasted Vegetable Minestrone

Roasting the vegetables for this minestrone brings out their caramelized sweetness, adding luxurious body and sophistication to this weeknight soup.

1   LARGE BULB FENNEL, CORED AND
    COARSELY CHOPPED

1   LARGE RED BELL PEPPER, SEEDED AND
    COARSELY CHOPPED

2   LARGE CARROTS, PEELED AND COARSELY
    CHOPPED

2   MEDIUM ZUCCHINI, TRIMMED AND DICED

1½ TABLESPOONS OLIVE OIL

¾   CUP UNCOOKED DITALINI OR OTHER
    SMALL-SHAPED PASTA

1   28-OUNCE CAN DICED TOMATOES,
    UNDRAINED

1   15-OUNCE CAN CANNELLONI OR OTHER
    WHITE BEANS, UNDRAINED

1   15-OUNCE CAN LIGHT RED KIDNEY BEANS,
    UNDRAINED

3   CUPS LOW-SODIUM CHICKEN
    OR VEGETABLE BROTH

1   TABLESPOON CHOPPED FRESH ROSEMARY

3   TABLESPOONS CHOPPED FRESH FLAT-LEAF
    PARSLEY LEAVES

½   CUP FRESHLY GRATED PARMESAN CHEESE,
    DIVIDED USE

Preheat the oven to 475°F. Line a rimmed baking sheet with foil.

In a large bowl toss the fennel, bell pepper, carrots, and zucchini with the oil. Season generously with salt and pepper. Spread on the prepared sheet. Roast the vegetables 25 minutes, turning every 8 minutes, until browned and tender.

While vegetables cook, bring a large saucepan of salted water to a boil. Add the pasta and cook until tender. Drain and rinse under cold water until cool.

Transfer the vegetables to the large saucepan used to boil the pasta. Add the tomatoes with their juices, the beans and their liquid, broth, and rosemary. Bring to a boil. Reduce heat to medium low, cover, and simmer for 20 minutes, stirring occasionally. Thin with water, if necessary, to get the consistency you like.

Stir in the cooked pasta, parsley, and ¼ cup of the cheese. Season with salt and pepper to taste. Serve sprinkled with the remaining cheese. **Makes 6 servings.**

60
MINUTES

NUTRITION PER SERVING:
CALORIES 212; FAT 5.1G (SAT 1.6G, MONO 1.1G, POLY 1.2G);
PROTEIN 9.6G; CHOLESTEROL 5.3MG; SODIUM 875MG; CARBOHYDRATE 36G.

Irish Cabbage Soup

Don't be misled by the plain-looking appearance of my riff on a classic Irish soup; it is thoroughly satisfying and delicious.

4	TEASPOONS UNSALTED BUTTER, DIVIDED USE	2	TEASPOONS KOSHER SALT
1½	CUPS CHOPPED ONION	½	TEASPOON FRESHLY GROUND BLACK PEPPER
2	LARGE YUKON GOLD POTATOES, PEELED AND CUT INTO ½-INCH PIECES	½	SMALL HEAD SAVOY CABBAGE, CORED, THINLY SLICED, AND CUT INTO ½-INCH PIECES
5½	CUPS LOW-SODIUM CHICKEN OR VEGETABLE BROTH	4	OUNCES SLICED CANADIAN BACON, COARSELY CHOPPED
4	TURKISH BAY LEAVES		

Melt 2 teaspoons of the butter in a large saucepan set over medium heat. Add the onion, then cook and stir until softened, about 5 minutes. Add the potatoes and cook and stir 2 minutes. Add the broth, bay leaves, salt, and pepper, and bring to a boil.

Reduce heat to medium low, cover, and simmer until the potatoes are soft, about 8 to 10 minutes. Add the cabbage and simmer 5 additional minutes.

Meanwhile, heat the remaining 2 teaspoons butter in a medium skillet over medium-high heat. Add the Canadian bacon and cook 3 to 4 minutes, until slightly crispy.

Discard the bay leaves from the soup. Transfer about one-third of the soup to a blender and purée until smooth. Return to the pot, stir in the bacon, and rewarm 2 minutes. Season with salt and pepper to taste. **Makes 6 servings.**

NUTRITION PER SERVING:
CALORIES 164; FAT 5.1G (SAT 2.1G, MONO 2.0G, POLY 0.8G);
PROTEIN 3.7G; CHOLESTEROL 6.0MG; SODIUM 345MG; CARBOHYDRATE 26.5G.

45 MINUTES

Dijon Vegetable Chowder

Creamy and rich—despite containing neither cream nor butter—this soup wards off winter with every spoonful. Don't skip the addition of the Dijon mustard—it adds tremendous flavor and depth in one easy step.

1 TABLESPOON OLIVE OIL

2 CUPS CHOPPED ONION

2 MEDIUM RED BELL PEPPERS, SEEDED AND DICED

2 TEASPOONS DRIED BASIL

3 CLOVES GARLIC, MINCED

3 CUPS 1% LOW-FAT MILK

3 CUPS LOW-SODIUM CHICKEN OR VEGETABLE BROTH

2 CUPS WATER

4 MEDIUM BAKING POTATOES (ABOUT 2½ POUNDS), PEELED AND CUT INTO ¾-INCH CUBES

1 16-OUNCE BAG FROZEN WHITE CORN

1 TABLESPOON DIJON MUSTARD

1 16-OUNCE BAG FROZEN CUT GREEN BEANS

Heat the oil in a large saucepan set over medium heat. Add the onion, bell peppers, and basil. Season with salt and pepper. Cook and stir 5 minutes. Add the garlic, milk, broth, water, and potatoes. Bring to a boil, then reduce the heat and simmer, covered, until the potatoes are almost tender, about 8 minutes.

Stir in the corn and simmer 2 minutes. With a slotted spoon, transfer 3 cups of the solids and 1 cup liquid to a blender. Add the mustard and purée until smooth. Return to the pot and add the green beans. Bring to a simmer, cooking 8 minutes or until the beans are tender. Season with salt and pepper to taste. **Makes 8 servings.**

NUTRITION PER SERVING:

CALORIES 142; FAT 4.9G (SAT 2.9G, MONO 1.0G, POLY 0.3G); PROTEIN 6.6G; CHOLESTEROL 15MG; SODIUM 509MG; CARBOHYDRATE 24.8G.

30 MINUTES

Japanese Soba Soup

WITH MISO & VEGETABLES

Soba noodles (brown Japanese noodles made from buckwheat), instant dashi (a powdered form of Japanese soup broth made from dried bonito tuna flakes and kombu), and miso (fermented soybean paste) can be found in the Asian foods section of well-stocked supermarkets. You can also find them quite easily at gourmet food purveyors, including Amazon.com.

½ POUND DRIED SOBA (BUCKWHEAT NOODLES)	1 10-OUNCE BAG PREWASHED SPINACH, COARSELY CHOPPED
8 CUPS WATER	¾ OF A 16-OUNCE PACKAGE FRESH SILKEN TOFU, DRAINED AND CUT INTO ½-INCH CUBES
4 TEASPOONS INSTANT POWDERED DASHI (DASHI-NO-MOTO)	
½ CUP LOW-SODIUM SOY SAUCE, PLUS ADDITIONAL TO TASTE	¼ CUP YELLOW MISO (FERMENTED BEAN PASTE) OR TO TASTE
3½ TEASPOONS SUGAR	2 GREEN ONIONS, TRIMMED AND CHOPPED
3 MEDIUM CARROTS, PEELED, AND CUT INTO THIN COINS	

Cook the soba noodles in a large pot of boiling salted water for 5 to 6 minutes, or until al dente (be careful not to overcook). Drain in colander and rinse under cold water until cool to the touch.

Place the water in a large saucepan set over high heat. Bring to a boil. Stir in the dashi. Reduce heat to low and cook, stirring occasionally, 3 minutes. Stir in the soy sauce and sugar. Cook 5 minutes.

Add the carrots. Cook 5 minutes. Stir in the spinach and tofu. Cook 1 minute. In a small bowl stir together the miso and ½ cup of the hot soup broth. Pour the mixture back into the pan. Season with additional soy sauce to taste.

Divide the noodles among 6 large bowls, ladle the soup over them, and sprinkle with equal amounts of the green onions. **Makes 6 servings.**

30 MINUTES

NUTRITION PER SERVING:
CALORIES 196; FAT 5.3G (SAT 0.8G, MONO 2.3G, POLY 2.5G); PROTEIN 14.1G; CHOLESTEROL 34MG; SODIUM 570MG; CARBOHYDRATE 28.2G.

Tuscan Bread Soup (Ribollita)

Ribollita is a hearty soup that provided Tuscans with a delicious way to use their leftovers (especially when times were lean). Ribollita literally translates as "reboiled," and traditionally the soup was always eaten two days in a row. In addition, the leftovers were poured into the bowl over a slice of stale bread, making use of old bread while thickening the soup. You don't have to serve this two days running, but the leftovers are indeed great.

3 CUPS CRUSTY COUNTRY BREAD CUBES	½ HEAD GREEN CABBAGE, HALVED AND THINLY SLICED CROSSWISE (ABOUT 6 CUPS)
2 TABLESPOONS OLIVE OIL	
1½ CUPS CHOPPED ONION	
3 MEDIUM CARROTS, HALVED LENGTHWISE AND CUT CROSSWISE ¼-INCH THICK	1 15-OUNCE CAN CANNELLINI OR OTHER WHITE BEANS, DRAINED
2 MEDIUM ZUCCHINI, TRIMMED AND SLICED	7 CUPS LOW-SODIUM CHICKEN OR VEGETABLE BROTH
4 CLOVES GARLIC, MINCED	
¼ CUP CANNED TOMATO PASTE	1 CUP CHOPPED FRESH PARSLEY LEAVES

Preheat oven to 300°F. Spread the bread in a single layer on a rimmed baking sheet. Bake until the pieces are dry, about 15 minutes. Remove from oven and set aside.

While the bread is toasting, heat the oil in a large saucepan set over medium-high heat. Add the onion, carrots, zucchini, and garlic. Season with salt and pepper. Cook and stir 8 minutes. Stir in the tomato paste. Cook and stir 1 minute.

Add the cabbage, beans, and broth. Simmer over medium heat 15 to 20 minutes, until soup is thickened. Season with salt and pepper to taste. Stir in the parsley. Divide the bread among six bowls and ladle the soup over. **Makes 6 servings.**

NUTRITION PER SERVING:
CALORIES 208; FAT 4.3G (SAT 0.7G, MONO 2.4G, POLY 1.8G);
PROTEIN 11.2G; CHOLESTEROL 2MG; SODIUM 397MG; CARBOHYDRATE 18.9G.

45 MINUTES

Winter Squash Soup

WITH CUMIN, KALE & BACON

When a dark, chilly autumn afternoon portends the first freezing night of fall, I head to the kitchen and begin making a steaming pot of this soup for dinner. Even my husband, who claims he does not like kale, loves this soup. (I think the bacon may have something to do with it.)

4 STRIPS BACON, CUT CROSSWISE INTO ½-INCH PIECES	2 12-OUNCE PACKAGES FROZEN (THAWED) WINTER SQUASH PURÉE
1¼ CUPS CHOPPED ONION	3½ CUPS LOW-SODIUM CHICKEN BROTH
½ POUND KALE, THICK STEMS REMOVED, LEAVES FINELY CHOPPED (ABOUT 8 CUPS)	2 TEASPOONS GROUND CUMIN
	½ TEASPOON CHIPOTLE CHILE POWDER

Cook the bacon in a large saucepan over medium heat, stirring occasionally, until crisp, 4 to 5 minutes. Using a slotted spoon, transfer the bacon to a paper-towel-lined plate. Drain all but 1 tablespoon fat from the pan.

Add the onion to the fat in the pan. Cook and stir 5 minutes. Add the kale. Cook 3 to 4 minutes, until the onion is soft.

Add the squash purée, broth, cumin, and chile powder. Bring to a boil, then reduce heat and simmer 2 minutes. Season with salt and pepper to taste. Serve garnished with reserved bacon. **Makes 6 servings.**

NUTRITION PER SERVING:
CALORIES 259; FAT 7.7G (SAT 2.6G, MONO 3.6G, POLY 1.4G);
PROTEIN 9.5G; CHOLESTEROL 11MG; SODIUM 679MG; CARBOHYDRATE 38.8G.

30 MINUTES

Peasant Soup

WITH BROCCOLI RABE, TOMATOES & CANNELLINI

I'd gladly eat this soup any day, even if it wasn't packed with nutrition. But loaded with nutrition it is, from the antioxidants and vitamins A and C in the broccoli rabe to the protein in the beans to the lycopene in the tomatoes. After cutting broccoli rabe as indicated in the recipe below, place it in a large bowl of cold water and agitate it to loosen the dirt. Lift the broccoli rabe from the bowl (leaving dirt and silt behind) and repeat if necessary.

2 15-OUNCE CANS CANNELLINI OR OTHER WHITE BEANS, RINSED AND DRAINED, DIVIDED USE	1 BUNCH (ABOUT 1 POUND) WELL-WASHED BROCCOLI RABE, CUT CROSSWISE 1 INCH THICK
1 TABLESPOON OLIVE OIL	4 CUPS LOW-SODIUM CHICKEN OR VEGETABLE BROTH
1¼ CUPS CHOPPED ONION	6 THICK SLICES RUSTIC WHOLE WHEAT BREAD, TOASTED
4 CLOVES GARLIC, MINCED	½ CUP FRESHLY GRATED PARMESAN CHEESE
3 TABLESPOONS TOMATO PASTE	
2 TABLESPOONS BALSAMIC VINEGAR	
2 TEASPOONS DRIED BASIL	
1 28-OUNCE CAN DICED TOMATOES, UNDRAINED	

Coarsely mash 1 can of the beans with a fork.

Heat the oil in a large saucepan over medium heat. Add the onion. Season with salt and pepper. Cook and stir 5 minutes. Add the garlic, tomato paste, vinegar, and basil. Cook and stir 2 minutes.

Add the mashed beans, remaining can of beans, tomatoes with their juices, broccoli rabe, and broth. Bring to a boil. Reduce heat to medium. Simmer, stirring occasionally, 8 to 10 minutes or until broccoli rabe is tender. Season with salt and pepper to taste.

To serve, place a slice of toasted bread in the bottom of each serving bowl. Ladle the soup over toast. Sprinkle with the Parmesan cheese. **Makes 6 servings.**

NUTRITION PER SERVING:
CALORIES 259; FAT 7.7G (SAT 2.6G, MONO 3.6G, POLY 1.4G);
PROTEIN 9.5G; CHOLESTEROL 11MG; SODIUM 579MG; CARBOHYDRATE 38.8G.

30 MINUTES

Winter Minestrone

WITH FENNEL, CHARD & POTATOES

This is one of my favorite midwinter soups, a hearty concoction—a cross between a soup and a stew—that relies on readily available winter vegetables. Though it doesn't take as long to make as the classic, it is countless times better than what you'll find in a can.

1 TABLESPOON OLIVE OIL	8 CUPS LOW-SODIUM CHICKEN OR VEGETABLE BROTH
1¼ CUPS CHOPPED ONION	1 15-OUNCE CAN CANNELLINI OR OTHER WHITE BEANS, RINSED AND DRAINED
2 RIBS CELERY, SLICED CROSSWISE INTO ½-INCH PIECES	1 CUP DITALINI OR OTHER SMALL-SHAPED PASTA
1½ CUPS CHOPPED FENNEL (ABOUT 1 MEDIUM BULB)	½ TEASPOON FRESHLY GROUND BLACK PEPPER
2 MEDIUM YUKON GOLD POTATOES, PEELED AND CUT INTO 1-INCH PIECES	2 TEASPOONS RED WINE VINEGAR
2 CLOVES GARLIC, FINELY CHOPPED	6 CUPS THINLY SLICED SWISS CHARD LEAVES
1 28-OUNCE CAN CRUSHED TOMATOES, UNDRAINED	OPTIONAL: FRESHLY GRATED PARMESAN CHEESE

Heat the oil in a large saucepan set over medium-high heat. Add the onion, celery, and fennel. Season with salt and pepper, then cook and stir 5 minutes. Add the potatoes and garlic. Cook and stir 2 minutes longer.

Add the tomatoes with their juices, broth, beans, pasta, and pepper. Increase heat to high and bring to a boil. Reduce the heat to low and simmer 10 to 12 minutes, until the potatoes and pasta are tender.

Stir in the vinegar and Swiss chard. Season with salt and pepper to taste. If desired, serve with the Parmesan cheese. **Makes 8 servings.**

NUTRITION PER SERVING:
CALORIES 140; FAT 1.6G (SAT 0.1G, MONO 0.5G, POLY 0.3G);
PROTEIN 6.8G; CHOLESTEROL 0MG; SODIUM 352MG; CARBOHYDRATE 25.1G.

45 MINUTES

Rustic Tomato Soup

WITH PASTA & PESTO

This is the soup I turn to when I'm craving something incredibly delicious for dinner, but don't feel like exerting much effort. It's so easy it practically makes itself. The ready-made marinara sauce and pesto make it taste like it's been cooking for hours (and that I've been slaving away, instead of propping up my feet). I know you'll love it, too.

1   TABLESPOON OLIVE OIL

2   LARGE CARROTS, PEELED AND CHOPPED

1   CUP CHOPPED ONION

1   CLOVE GARLIC, MINCED

1   26-OUNCE JAR GOOD-QUALITY MARINARA
    SAUCE

3½ CUPS LOW-SODIUM CHICKEN OR
    VEGETABLE BROTH

1   15-OUNCE CAN CANNELLINI OR OTHER
    WHITE BEANS, RINSED AND DRAINED

½   TEASPOON RED PEPPER FLAKES

½   CUP ORZO OR OTHER VERY SMALL-SHAPED
    PASTA

¼   CUP PREPARED REFRIGERATED PESTO

Heat the oil in a large saucepan set over medium-high heat. Add the carrots and onion. Season with salt and pepper. Cook and stir 5 minutes. Add the garlic and cook and stir 1 minute longer.

Stir in the marinara sauce, broth, beans, and red pepper flakes. Bring to a boil, then reduce heat and simmer 10 minutes, until the pasta is al dente. Season with salt and pepper to taste. Serve the soup drizzled with the pesto. **Makes 6 servings.**

NUTRITION PER SERVING:
CALORIES 205; FAT 6.7G (SAT 2.1G, MONO 2.8G, POLY 1.3G);
PROTEIN 11.4G; CHOLESTEROL 8MG; SODIUM 578MG; CARBOHYDRATE 27.1G.

30 MINUTES

Smoky Corn Chowder

This soup is particularly delicious when made with sweet white corn, but I love the color of yellow corn. My solution? One bag of white corn, one bag of yellow. I make this soup year-round—it seems to suit every season, and because the ingredients come from the pantry and freezer, it's convenient for anytime cooking and eating. And while it is quick and simple enough for weeknights, it is impressive as a first course at the Thanksgiving table, too.

4 SLICES BACON, CUT INTO ½-INCH PIECES	3 CUPS LOW-SODIUM CHICKEN OR VEGETABLE BROTH
1½ CUPS CHOPPED ONION	1 CUP CANNED FAT-FREE EVAPORATED MILK (FROM A 12-OUNCE CAN)
2 CLOVES GARLIC, FINELY CHOPPED	
½ TEASPOON HOT SMOKED PAPRIKA	4 GREEN ONIONS, TRIMMED AND THINLY SLICED
½ TEASPOON GROUND CUMIN	
2 10-OUNCE PACKAGES FROZEN CORN (WHITE OR YELLOW)	

Cook the bacon in a large saucepan set over medium heat until crisp, about 8 minutes. Transfer to a paper-towel-lined plate.

Discard all but 1 tablespoon of the drippings and return the pot to medium heat. Add the onion. Cook and stir 7 minutes. Add the garlic, paprika, and cumin and cook, stirring, for 2 minutes. Stir in the corn and broth, and bring to a boil. Reduce heat and simmer 15 minutes.

Transfer half the soup to a blender and purée until smooth. Return the purée to the saucepan and stir to combine. Stir in the milk and season with salt and pepper to taste. Heat 1 minute longer. Serve topped with the green onions and bacon. **Makes 6 servings.**

NUTRITION PER SERVING:
CALORIES 188; FAT 6.1G (SAT 3.0G, MONO 1.6G, POLY 1.1G);
PROTEIN 11.1G; CHOLESTEROL 28MG; SODIUM 294MG; CARBOHYDRATE 23G.

45 MINUTES

Garlicky Spinach & Tomato Soup

WITH CHEESE RAVIOLI

This is one of those recipes whose sum is far greater than its parts. The garlic and basil infuse the ready-made broth with deep flavor, while the spinach and ravioli offer delicious and filling substance. If you can find fire-roasted tomatoes (e.g., Muir Glen brand), use them—they add a smoky nuance to the soup that's smashing. If you use regular tomatoes, consider adding ¼ teaspoon ground cumin to the broth; it will deliver a similarly subtle smokiness. This soup's best feature, though, may be that it is loved by all, including infants, adults, and picky teenagers.

1 TABLESPOON OLIVE OIL	2 5-OUNCE BAGS PREWASHED BABY
8 CLOVES GARLIC, CHOPPED	SPINACH, WASHED, STEMMED, AND
6 CUPS LOW-SODIUM CHICKEN	COARSELY CHOPPED
OR VEGETABLE BROTH	12 BASIL LEAVES, COARSELY CHOPPED
1 9-OUNCE PACKAGE FRESH OR FROZEN	OPTIONAL: FRESHLY GRATED PARMESAN
CHEESE RAVIOLI	CHEESE
1 14.5-OUNCE CAN DICED TOMATOES,	
UNDRAINED (PREFERABLY FIRE-ROASTED)	

Heat the oil in a large saucepan over medium-high heat. Add the garlic. Cook and stir 1 to 2 minutes, until the garlic softens.

Add the broth to the pan. Bring to a boil. Add the ravioli and cook 5 minutes for frozen pasta, 2 minutes for fresh (the pasta will be partially cooked).

Add the tomatoes with their juices. Reduce heat to low and simmer 3 to 5 minutes longer, until the ravioli is tender. Stir in the spinach and basil and cook 1 to 2 minutes, until wilted. Season with salt and pepper to taste. Serve sprinkled with the Parmesan cheese, if desired. **Makes 6 servings.**

NUTRITION PER SERVING:
CALORIES 206; FAT 7.9G (SAT 3.2G, MONO 2.6G, POLY 1.2G); PROTEIN 8.4G; CHOLESTEROL 41MG; SODIUM 603MG; CARBOHYDRATE 23.3G.

20 MINUTES

Curried Couscous, Spinach & Roasted Tomato Soup

How could something so easy to make taste so complex and exotic? This little soup pulls it off, all while packing in a slew of good-for-you ingredients, too. Israeli couscous is toasted semolina pasta; each grain is about half the size of a green pea. Even in hot soup, this kind of couscous retains al dente firmness for a long time. If you can't find it, use another variety of tiny pasta, such as orzo or riso.

2 TEASPOONS UNSALTED BUTTER	1 14.5-OUNCE CAN FIRE-ROASTED TOMATOES
1 CUP CHOPPED ONION	(E.G., MUIR GLEN BRAND), UNDRAINED
½ CUP UNCOOKED ISRAELI COUSCOUS	4½ CUPS LOW-SODIUM CHICKEN OR
1½ TEASPOONS CURRY POWDER	VEGETABLE BROTH
1 GARLIC CLOVE, MINCED	1 6-OUNCE PACKAGE PREWASHED BABY
	SPINACH

Melt the butter in a large saucepan over medium-high heat. Add the onion. Season with salt and pepper. Cook and stir 5 minutes. Add the couscous, curry, and garlic, then cook and stir 3 minutes.

Add the tomatoes with their juices and broth. Bring to a boil. Reduce the heat, and simmer 7 minutes or until the couscous is almost tender. Stir in the spinach and cook 1 to 2 minutes, until wilted. Season with salt and pepper to taste. **Makes 4 servings.**

NUTRITION PER SERVING:
CALORIES 169; FAT 5.6G (SAT 1.6G, MONO 3.1G, POLY 0.6G);
PROTEIN 4.7G; CHOLESTEROL 6MG; SODIUM 446MG; CARBOHYDRATE 25.1G.

20 MINUTES

Punjabi Potato & Cauliflower Soup

WITH MINTED YOGURT

A fragrant curry broth, bright with the flavors of lime and fresh spinach, brings an Indian accent to familiar potatoes. The minted yogurt is a must, adding a cool, creamy contrast to the spice.

⅔ CUP PLAIN LOW-FAT YOGURT

2 GREEN ONIONS, ENDS TRIMMED AND THINLY SLICED

2 TABLESPOONS CHOPPED FRESH MINT LEAVES

1 TABLESPOON OLIVE OIL

1 HEAD CAULIFLOWER, BROKEN INTO FLO-RETS (ABOUT 4 CUPS)

1 CUP CHOPPED ONION

1 POUND YUKON GOLD POTATOES, PEELED AND CUT INTO ½-INCH CUBES (ABOUT 3 CUPS)

1½ TABLESPOONS MILD CURRY POWDER

1 TEASPOON GROUND CUMIN

1 TEASPOON GROUND GINGER

2 CLOVES GARLIC, MINCED

4½ CUPS LOW-SODIUM VEGETABLE BROTH

1 5-OUNCE BAG PREWASHED BABY SPINACH

JUICE AND GRATED ZEST OF 2 LIMES

1 14- TO 16-OUNCE CONTAINER EXTRA-FIRM TOFU, DRAINED, CUT INTO ½-INCH CUBES

In a small bowl mix the yogurt, green onions, and mint. Cover and chill.

Heat the oil in a large saucepan set over high heat. Add the cauliflower and onion, then season with salt and pepper. Cook and stir until the onion and cauliflower begin to brown, stirring often, about 5 minutes. Add the potatoes and stir 2 minutes. Add the curry powder, cumin, ginger, and garlic and stir 1 minute.

Add the broth. Bring to a boil. Reduce the heat to medium, cover, and simmer 10 minutes or until the vegetables are tender. Stir in the spinach and cook 1 to 2 minutes, until wilted.

Add the lime juice, lime zest, and tofu. Cook 2 minutes longer. Season with salt and pepper to taste. Serve topped with dollops of the minted yogurt. **Makes 6 servings.**

NUTRITION PER SERVING:
CALORIES 171; FAT 3.5G (SAT 0.8G, MONO 2.4G, POLY 0.2G);
PROTEIN 11.1G; CHOLESTEROL 0MG; SODIUM 529MG; CARBOHYDRATE 25G.

30 MINUTES

Soupe au Pistou

Pistou is a Provençal variant of pesto made of basil, garlic, olive oil, and salt; soupe au pistou is a hearty vegetable soup with the pistou stirred right in before serving. Here I've lightened the pistou (using a fraction of the olive oil) without any sacrifice of flavor. When the pistou is stirred in, the soup turns a vibrant green and becomes perfumed with the intense, sweet aroma of basil mixed with garlic.

1	14.5-OUNCE CAN DICED TOMATOES, DRAINED, DIVIDED USE	8	CUPS LOW-SODIUM CHICKEN OR VEGETABLE BROTH, DIVIDED USE
2	CUPS PACKED FRESH BASIL LEAVES	½	CUP ORZO (RICE-SHAPED PASTA) (OR OTHER TINY-SHAPED PASTA)
3	TABLESPOONS FRESHLY GRATED PARMESAN CHEESE	1½	CUPS FRESH OR FROZEN CUT GREEN BEANS
2	TABLESPOONS OLIVE OIL	1	15-OUNCE CAN WHITE BEANS (ANY VARIETY), RINSED AND DRAINED
3	CLOVES GARLIC, ROUGHLY CHOPPED	¼	TEASPOON DRIED CRUSHED RED PEPPER
2	LARGE LEEKS (WHITE AND PALE GREEN PARTS ONLY), CHOPPED AND RINSED		OPTIONAL: FRESHLY GRATED PARMESAN CHEESE
2	MEDIUM CARROTS, PEELED AND CHOPPED		
1	MEDIUM YUKON GOLD POTATO, PEELED AND DICED		

Measure ½ cup of the drained tomatoes and place in a food processor with the basil, Parmesan cheese, oil, and garlic. Purée. Season the pistou with salt and pepper.

Combine the leeks, carrots, potato, and 1 cup of the broth in a large saucepan set over medium-low heat. Cook until the vegetables are almost tender, stirring occasionally, about 8 minutes.

Add the remaining broth. Bring to a boil. Stir in the orzo. Bring to a boil, then reduce heat to medium. Simmer, uncovered, 12 minutes, until the orzo is almost tender, stirring often. Add the green beans, white beans, red pepper, and remaining tomatoes. Cook 10 minutes. Season with salt and pepper to taste.

Stir the pistou into the soup and serve. If desired, sprinkle with the additional Parmesan cheese. **Makes 6 servings.**

45 MINUTES

NUTRITION PER SERVING:
CALORIES 211; FAT 4.3G (SAT 1.6G, MONO 1.3G, POLY 1.4G);
PROTEIN 9.1G; CHOLESTEROL 5MG; SODIUM 303MG; CARBOHYDRATE 34G.

Hominy, Tomato & Chile Soup

Whenever I feel the sniffles coming on, I turn to this satisfying soup. I figure that with its ample spices, broth, tomatoes, and herbs, plus its soothing heat, it must be doing something to make me feel better. But even when I'm not sick, I still savor this soup. I'm something of a hominy cheerleader. It's a quick and convenient ingredient for adding heft to a soup (without any prep work), and it typically costs a mere 75 cents per can. The flavor is reminiscent of freshly baked corn tortillas (what can beat that?), which harmonizes with Mexican and Southwestern flavors. It is available at most every supermarket, right next to the canned corn.

1	TABLESPOON OLIVE OIL	1	4-OUNCE CAN DICED GREEN CHILES
1	CUP CHOPPED ONION	1	15-OUNCE CAN GOLDEN HOMINY, DRAINED
3	CLOVES GARLIC, MINCED	1	14.5-OUNCE CAN DICED TOMATOES, UNDRAINED
1	TABLESPOON CHILI POWDER		
1½	TEASPOONS GROUND CUMIN	⅓	CUP FINELY CRUSHED BAKED TORTILLA CHIPS
1	TEASPOON DRIED OREGANO		
4	CUPS LOW-SODIUM CHICKEN OR VEGETABLE BROTH	1	TO 2 TABLESPOONS FRESH LIME JUICE
		¼	CUP CHOPPED FRESH CILANTRO LEAVES

Heat the oil in a large saucepan set over medium-high heat. Add the onion. Season with salt and pepper, then cook and stir 5 minutes. Add the garlic, chili powder, cumin, and oregano. Cook and stir 1 minute.

Add the broth, green chiles, hominy, tomatoes with their juices, and crushed tortilla chips. Bring to a boil. Reduce heat to medium low. Simmer, covered, 15 minutes to blend flavors. Season the soup with salt and pepper to taste. Stir in 1 to 2 tablespoons lime juice, to taste. Serve sprinkled with the chopped cilantro. **Makes 6 servings.**

NUTRITION PER SERVING:
CALORIES 148; FAT 3.4G (SAT 0.8G, MONO 0.8G, POLY 1.7G);
PROTEIN 6.1G; CHOLESTEROL 15MG; SODIUM 764MG; CARBOHYDRATE 40.1G.

30 MINUTES

Chinese-Style Bok Choy & Mushroom Soup

If you're not familiar with bok choy, it's time to get acquainted. It may sound exotic, but this mild, versatile vegetable with crunchy white stalks and tender, dark-green leaves is commonly available and well priced at most supermarkets (including my tiny-town Texas one). What makes it worth knowing is twofold: taste and nutrition. It has a light, sweet flavor and crisp texture that comes from its high water content. That high water content makes it perfect for fast, flavorful soups because it takes just minutes for it to wilt. As for nutrition, bok choy is very high in vitamin A, vitamin C, calcium, and fiber, and very low in calories.

1 POUND BABY BOK CHOY (ABOUT 5 TO 8 HEADS)	1 TABLESPOON MINCED PEELED FRESH GINGER
6 CUPS LOW-SODIUM CHICKEN OR VEGETABLE BROTH	1 16-OUNCE PACKAGE SLICED WHITE MUSHROOMS
2 TABLESPOONS LOW-SODIUM SOY SAUCE	½ OF A 14- TO 16-OUNCE PACKAGE FIRM TOFU, CUT INTO ½-INCH PIECES
2 TABLESPOONS RICE VINEGAR	
1 TABLESPOON ASIAN TOASTED SESAME OIL	3 GREEN ONIONS, ENDS TRIMMED AND CHOPPED
3 CLOVES GARLIC, MINCED	

Remove any bruised or withered outer leaves from the bok choy. Trim ⅛ inch from the bottom of each bok choy, then cut each head into quarters. Wash the bok choy in several changes of cold water. Drain.

Combine the broth, soy sauce, vinegar, sesame oil, garlic and ginger in a large saucepan set over medium-high heat. Bring to a boil, then add the mushrooms. Reduce heat to low and simmer 5 minutes or until the mushrooms are tender.

Add the tofu, bok choy, and green onions. Simmer until the bok choy wilts and the tofu is heated through, about 3 to 4 minutes. Season the soup with additional soy sauce to taste. **Makes 4 servings.**

NUTRITION PER SERVING:
CALORIES 89; FAT 3.7G (SAT 1.9G, MONO 1.0G, POLY 0.7G);
PROTEIN 6.1G; CHOLESTEROL 0MG; SODIUM 278MG; CARBOHYDRATE 11.7G.

20 MINUTES

Dutch Farmer's Cheese & Vegetable Soup

This take on a traditional Dutch soup, warm with winter vegetables, bread, and cheese, may be the ultimate comfort food. I like to think of it as a grilled cheese sandwich and hearty vegetable soup all in one.

1 TABLESPOON UNSALTED BUTTER	1 POUND CARROTS, PEELED AND SLICED
1½ TEASPOONS CARAWAY SEEDS, CRUSHED SLIGHTLY	1 CUP CHOPPED ONION
	6 CUPS LOW-SODIUM CHICKEN OR
1½ POUNDS RUSSET POTATOES, PEELED AND DICED	VEGETABLE BROTH
	6 1-INCH-THICK FRENCH BREAD SLICES
1 CAULIFLOWER HEAD (ABOUT ½ POUND), TRIMMED, CUT INTO FLORETS	1½ CUPS SHREDDED SMOKED GOUDA CHEESE

Melt the butter in a heavy, large saucepan set over medium-high heat. Add the caraway, potatoes, cauliflower, carrots, and onion. Cook and stir until the onion is golden brown and the vegetables are beginning to brown at the edges, about 10 minutes.

Add the broth to the pan and bring to a boil. Reduce heat to medium low. Simmer, covered, until vegetables are tender, adding small amounts of water if the soup is too thick, about 20 to 25 minutes.

Transfer 1½ cups of the vegetables and 1 cup broth to a blender, then process until smooth. Return to the saucepan, stirring to blend. Season with salt and pepper to taste.

Preheat the broiler, positioning a rack 6 inches from the heat. Arrange the bread in single layer on a baking sheet, then sprinkle each with ¼ cup Gouda cheese. Place in the oven and broil just until the cheese melts and is golden, watching closely to avoid burning, about 1 minute.

Serve the soup in bowls topped with a slice of the cheese bread, cheese side up. **Makes 6 servings.**

NUTRITION PER SERVING:
CALORIES 178; FAT 4.6G (SAT 2.6G, MONO 1.4G, POLY 0.3G); PROTEIN 6.6G; CHOLESTEROL 12MG; SODIUM 464MG; CARBOHYDRATE 20.6G.

60 MINUTES

Spicy Sweet Potato & Coconut Soup

Combining sweet potatoes and coconut may sound unusual, but it's actually quite common in a number of cuisines, including those from Southeast Asia and the Caribbean. My take is a cross between the two. Fresh ginger and Thai red curry paste impart exotic notes, and fresh lime juice and cilantro provide bright contrast to the rich coconut broth.

1½ POUNDS RED-SKINNED SWEET POTATOES (YAMS), PEELED AND CUT INTO 1-INCH PIECES

1 TABLESPOON CANOLA OIL

1 CUP CHOPPED ONION

3 TABLESPOONS PEELED, MINCED FRESH GINGER

1 TABLESPOON THAI RED CURRY PASTE

1 14-OUNCE CAN UNSWEETENED LIGHT COCONUT MILK

3 CUPS LOW-SODIUM CHICKEN OR VEGETABLE BROTH

3½ TABLESPOONS LIME JUICE

1 TABLESPOON TOASTED SESAME OIL

½ CUP FRESH CILANTRO LEAVES

Bring a large saucepan of water to a boil over high heat. Add the sweet potatoes and cook until tender, about 20 minutes. Drain.

Heat the oil in the same saucepan over medium heat. Add the onion. Season with salt and pepper, then cook and stir 5 minutes. Stir in the ginger and curry paste and cook 1 minute.

Add the coconut milk, broth, and sweet potatoes and bring to a boil. Reduce heat to low and simmer, partially covered, 10 minutes.

Stir in the lime juice and season with salt and pepper to taste. Serve the soup drizzled with the sesame oil and sprinkled with the cilantro. **Makes 4 servings.**

NUTRITION PER SERVING:
CALORIES 191; FAT 2.8G (SAT 1.6G, MONO 0.7G, POLY 0.2G);
PROTEIN 5.1G; CHOLESTEROL 7MG; SODIUM 565MG; CARBOHYDRATE 19.7G.

60 MINUTES

Vegetable Tortellini Soup

WITH ASPARAGUS, PEAS & PARMESAN

Sure, there's nothing wrong with your basic vegetable soup, but vegetable soup made with tender tortellini and spring vegetables, enveloped in a lemon-and-herb broth and topped with nutty Parmesan cheese, gives this family favorite a new and very delicious angle.

8 CUPS LOW-SODIUM CHICKEN OR
  VEGETABLE BROTH
½ CUP CHOPPED FLAT-LEAF PARSLEY LEAVES,
  DIVIDED USE
JUICE AND GRATED ZEST OF 1 LARGE LEMON,
  DIVIDED USE
1 9-OUNCE PACKAGE REFRIGERATED
  CHEESE-FILLED TORTELLINI

¾ POUND ASPARAGUS, TRIMMED AND THINLY
  SLICED DIAGONALLY, LEAVING TIPS INTACT
1½ CUPS FROZEN BABY GREEN PEAS
  (APPROXIMATELY HALF OF A 1-POUND
  BAG, UNTHAWED)
⅓ CUP FRESHLY GRATED PARMESAN CHEESE

Place the broth, ¼ cup of the parsley, and lemon zest in a large saucepan set over medium-high heat. Bring to a boil, then reduce heat to medium low. Add the tortellini and cook 3 minutes.

Add the asparagus and peas, and simmer, uncovered, 4 to 5 minutes longer, until the tortellini is cooked through and the asparagus is crisp-tender.

Stir in the lemon juice and season with salt and pepper to taste. Serve, sprinkled with the Parmesan cheese and the remaining parsley. **Makes 6 servings.**

NUTRITION PER SERVING:
CALORIES 216; FAT 7.2G (SAT 2.3G, MONO 3.5G, POLY 0.7G);
PROTEIN 12.1G; CHOLESTEROL 25MG; SODIUM 574MG; CARBOHYDRATE 32.1G.

20 MINUTES

Green Chile Chowder

Ready-packed diced green chiles are an easy and delicious way to incorporate the rich, full flavor of poblanos into speedy dishes such as my green chile chowder. Poblanos are mild, not hot, so I've added smoky heat to the soup with another chile, chipotles. Don't worry about too much heat—it's mellowed by the milk and potatoes. A fresh batch of cornbread is the perfect accompaniment.

1 TABLESPOON CANOLA OIL	1 TEASPOON CHIPOTLE CHILE POWDER (OR
1¼ CUPS CHOPPED ONION	TO TASTE)
2 CUPS FROZEN (THAWED) WHITE CORN	1 TEASPOON SALT
KERNELS, DIVIDED USE	1 12-OUNCE CAN EVAPORATED FAT-FREE
2½ CUPS 1% LOW-FAT MILK, DIVIDED USE	MILK
1¼ POUNDS RUSSET BAKING POTATOES,	2 4-OUNCE CANS DICED GREEN CHILES
PEELED AND DICED	⅔ CUP CHOPPED FRESH CILANTRO LEAVES,
2 TEASPOONS GROUND CUMIN	DIVIDED USE

Heat the oil in a large saucepan over medium heat. Add the onion. Season with salt and pepper. Cook and stir 5 minutes.

Purée 1 cup of the corn with 1 cup of the 1% milk in a blender. Pour the mixture into the pan with the onion. Stir in the remaining 1% milk and corn and add the potatoes, cumin, chile powder, and salt. Reduce the heat to medium low and cook 12 to 15 minutes or until the potatoes are very tender.

Stir in the evaporated milk, green chiles, and half of the cilantro. Heat through, about 2 minutes. Season with salt and pepper to taste. Serve sprinkled with the remaining cilantro. **Makes 6 servings.**

NUTRITION PER SERVING:
CALORIES 96; FAT 2.8G (SAT 1.3G, MONO 0.6G, POLY 0.3G);
PROTEIN 4.7G; CHOLESTEROL 6.9MG; SODIUM 497MG; CARBOHYDRATE 15.1G.

30 MINUTES

3. POULTRY

Soups

Home-style Chicken Soup, Chicken Noodle Soup, Chicken & Rice Soup, Chicken & Cheese Ravioli Soup, Chicken, Gnocchi & Spring Pea Soup, Lemony Chicken, Tomato & Fennel Soup with Gorgonzola, Cajun Chicken & Vegetable Soup, Harira (Moroccan Chicken Soup with Chickpeas & Lentils), Lemon Chicken Soup with Fresh Spinach & Pasta, Italian Tortellini-Sausage Soup, Rice Congee Soup (Jook), Chicken Posole, Tortilla Chicken Soup, Chunky Turkey Vegetable Soup with Sweet Potatoes & Greens, Asian Chicken Noodle Soup, Gingered Chicken & Vegetable Soup, West African Spicy Chicken & Peanut Soup, Country Captain Soup, Ajiaco (Potato, Corn, and Chicken Soup), Chicken Chowder with Cheddar Cheese & Bacon, Turkey & Wild Rice Soup, Thai Chicken & Coconut Soup, Chicken & Couscous Soup with Exotic Spices, Golden Turkey Soup with Corn & Orzo, Chipotle Chicken Chowder, Turkey Curry Soup

Home-style Chicken Soup

Warming and old-fashioned, this ever-comforting soup gets to the table in a flash thanks to store-bought rotisserie chicken. The variations are limited only by your imagination; I've provided a few of my favorites to get you started.

1	STORE-BOUGHT ROTISSERIE CHICKEN	2	LARGE CELERY RIBS, TRIMMED AND THINLY SLICED
1	TABLESPOON OLIVE OIL	1	TEASPOON DRIED THYME LEAVES
2	CUPS CHOPPED ONION	8	CUPS LOW-SODIUM CHICKEN BROTH
2	LARGE CARROTS, PEELED, HALVED LENGTHWISE, AND THINLY SLICED		

Remove the chicken meat from the chicken, discarding bones and skin. Cut or shred the chicken meat into bite-size pieces (approximately 4 cups).

Heat the oil in a large saucepan set over medium-high heat. Add the onion, carrots, and celery. Season with salt and pepper to taste. Cook and stir 8 minutes. Add the chicken, thyme, and broth. Bring to a simmer and cook 5 minutes to blend flavors. **Makes 8 servings.**

Variations (Add any of the options to the prepared soup. Simmer 15 minutes longer.)

Chicken Noodle Soup: 3 cups egg noodles, 1 cup frozen petite peas, and ½ cup chopped fresh parsley.

Chicken & Rice Soup: ¼ cup uncooked long grain white rice, 1 cup frozen petite peas, and ½ cup chopped fresh flat-leaf parsley.

Chicken & Cheese Ravioli Soup: 1 9-ounce package refrigerated cheese ravioli; 1 14.5-ounce can diced tomatoes, undrained; 2 medium zucchini, diced; 1 teaspoon dried basil; ½ cup chopped fresh basil.

Chicken, Gnocchi & Spring Pea Soup: 1 16-ounce package potato gnocchi, 1½ cups frozen petite peas, 2 tablespoons fresh lemon juice, and ½ cup chopped fresh flat-leaf parsley.

NUTRITION PER SERVING:
CALORIES 181; FAT 5.2G (SAT 3.1G, MONO 1.1G, POLY 0.9G);
PROTEIN 25.2G; CHOLESTEROL 5MG; SODIUM 702MG; CARBOHYDRATE 10.1G.

Lemony Chicken, Tomato & Fennel Soup

WITH GORGONZOLA

There is something so satisfying about melted cheese, whether on bread, pasta, or even atop a big bowl of homemade soup, as it's found here. This soup is at once fresh and comforting; the hint of licorice from the fennel bulb and chopped fennel fronds magically elevates the entire dish from ordinary to extraordinary.

2 TEASPOONS OLIVE OIL	⅓ CUP TINY STAR OR RICE-SHAPED PASTA
1 MEDIUM FENNEL, TRIMMED AND CHOPPED BULB (RESERVE FRONDS FOR GARNISH)	3 CUPS DICED OR SHREDDED COOKED CHICKEN (E.G., FROM A PURCHASED ROTISSERIE CHICKEN)
3 CLOVES GARLIC, MINCED	2 TABLESPOONS FRESH LEMON JUICE
2 CUPS LOW-SODIUM CHICKEN BROTH	½ CUP (2 OUNCES) CRUMBLED GORGONZOLA CHEESE
1 28-OUNCE CAN CRUSHED TOMATOES, UNDRAINED	
1 TEASPOON GRATED LEMON ZEST	

Heat the oil in a large saucepan set over medium-high heat. Add the fennel bulb. Season with salt and pepper. Cook and stir 5 minutes. Add the garlic. Cook and stir 1 minute.

Add the broth, tomatoes with their juices, and lemon zest. Bring to a boil. Add the pasta. Reduce heat to medium, partially cover, and cook 6 to 7 minutes, until the pasta is tender. Add the chicken and lemon juice. Cook 5 minutes to blend flavors. Season with salt and pepper to taste.

Mince the reserved fennel fronds. Serve the soup sprinkled with the cheese and fennel fronds. **Makes 4 servings.**

NUTRITION PER SERVING:
CALORIES 254; FAT 8.4G (SAT 4.1G, MONO 2.0G, POLY 0.9G); PROTEIN 16.3G; CHOLESTEROL 85MG; SODIUM 699MG; CARBOHYDRATE 11.8G.

30 MINUTES

Cajun Chicken & Vegetable Soup

This beautiful soup features a classic combination of Cajun flavors. Though lightened to be healthier, it is still rich and zesty.

1½ TABLESPOONS CANOLA OIL	1 14.5-OUNCE CAN DICED TOMATOES, UNDRAINED
2 TABLESPOONS ALL-PURPOSE FLOUR	
2 MEDIUM RED BELL PEPPERS, SEEDED AND CHOPPED	1 10-OUNCE PACKAGE FROZEN CUT OKRA, UNTHAWED
1 CUP CHOPPED ONION	½ OF A 16-OUNCE PACKAGE LIGHT SMOKED SAUSAGE, DICED
4 CLOVES GARLIC, MINCED	
1 TABLESPOON HOT SAUCE	2 CUPS DICED OR SHREDDED COOKED CHICKEN BREAST (E.G., FROM A PURCHASED ROTISSERIE CHICKEN)
1½ TEASPOONS DRIED THYME LEAVES	
1 TEASPOON DRIED OREGANO	
5 CUPS LOW-SODIUM CHICKEN BROTH	

Heat the oil in a large saucepan set over medium heat. Add the flour and cook 4 to 5 minutes, stirring constantly, until light brown. Stir in the bell peppers, onion, garlic, hot sauce, thyme, and oregano. Season with salt and pepper. Cook and stir 5 minutes.

Add the broth, tomatoes with their juices, and okra. Bring to a boil. Reduce heat to medium low, partially cover, and simmer 10 minutes.

Stir in the sausage and chicken. Cook 5 minutes to warm through and blend flavors. Season with salt and pepper to taste. **Makes 6 servings.**

NUTRITION PER SERVING:
CALORIES 205; FAT 5.1G (SAT 1.5G, MONO 1.7G, POLY 1.5G);
PROTEIN 18.4G; CHOLESTEROL 56MG; SODIUM 634MG; CARBOHYDRATE 27G.

30 MINUTES

Harira

(MOROCCAN CHICKEN SOUP WITH CHICKPEAS & LENTILS)

Whenever I'm developing a cookbook, some recipes stand out from all the others and become instant favorites. Harira, a traditional Moroccan soup, is one such recipe. Not just another chicken soup, it's simple, hearty, and spectacularly delicious.

1 TABLESPOON OLIVE OIL	½ CUP UNCOOKED LONG GRAIN RICE
2 CUPS CHOPPED ONION	½ CUP LENTILS
1 TABLESPOON GROUND CUMIN	3 CUPS DICED OR SHREDDED COOKED
2 TEASPOONS GROUND GINGER	CHICKEN (E.G., FROM A PURCHASED
8 CUPS LOW-SODIUM CHICKEN BROTH	ROTISSERIE CHICKEN)
1 28-OUNCE CAN CRUSHED TOMATOES,	¾ CUP FINELY CHOPPED FRESH CILANTRO
UNDRAINED	LEAVES
¼ TEASPOON CRUMBLED SAFFRON THREADS	¾ CUP FINELY CHOPPED FRESH FLAT-LEAF
1 15-OUNCE CAN CHICKPEAS (GARBANZO	PARSLEY LEAVES
BEANS), RINSED AND DRAINED	

Heat the oil in a large saucepan set over medium-high heat. Add the onion. Season with salt and pepper. Cook and stir 5 minutes. Add the cumin and ginger. Cook and stir 30 seconds.

Add the broth, tomatoes with their juices, saffron, chickpeas, rice, and lentils. Reduce heat to low, cover, and cook 30 to 35 minutes, until the lentils are tender. Stir in the chicken and season with salt and pepper to taste. Just before serving, stir in the cilantro and parsley. **Makes 8 servings.**

NUTRITION PER SERVING:
CALORIES 258; FAT 7.4G (SAT 2.1G, MONO 3.1G, POLY 1.9G);
PROTEIN 21.5G; CHOLESTEROL 76MG; SODIUM 332MG; CARBOHYDRATE 28.2G.

45 MINUTES

Lemon Chicken Soup

WITH FRESH SPINACH & PASTA

Even if it's still chilly outside, several spoonfuls of this bright and colorful soup will make you feel spring is in the air.

1 TABLESPOON OLIVE OIL	2 CUPS COOKED DICED OR SHREDDED
1½ CUPS CHOPPED ONION	COOKED CHICKEN (E.G., FROM A PUR-
2 CLOVES GARLIC, MINCED	CHASED ROTISSERIE CHICKEN)
1½ TEASPOONS GROUND CUMIN	¼ CUP FRESH LEMON JUICE
4 MEDIUM CARROTS, PEELED AND DICED	2 TEASPOONS GRATED LEMON ZEST
1 LARGE RED BELL PEPPER, SEEDED AND	½ OF A 10-OUNCE PACKAGE PREWASHED
DICED	SPINACH
8 CUPS LOW-SODIUM CHICKEN BROTH	½ CUP FRESHLY GRATED PARMESAN CHEESE
2 CUPS UNCOOKED FARFALLE (BOW-TIE	
PASTA)	

Heat the oil in a large saucepan set over medium-high heat. Add the onion. Season with salt and pepper. Cook and stir 5 minutes. Add the garlic and cumin. Cook and stir 1 minute. Add the carrots and red bell pepper. Cook and stir 7 to 8 minutes.

Add the broth to the pan. Bring to a boil. Add the pasta. Cook 10 to 12 minutes, stirring occasionally, until the pasta is tender. Reduce the heat to medium low.

Add the chicken, lemon juice, lemon zest, and spinach to the pan. Simmer 3 minutes, until the spinach wilts but is still bright green. Season with salt and pepper to taste. Serve sprinkled with the Parmesan cheese. **Makes 8 servings.**

NUTRITION PER SERVING:
CALORIES 246; FAT 4.9G (SAT 2.1G, MONO 1.9G, POLY 0.5G);
PROTEIN 24.1G; CHOLESTEROL 21MG; SODIUM 642MG; CARBOHYDRATE 27G.

45 MINUTES

Italian Tortellini-Sausage Soup

Plump pillows of cheese tortellini hold their shape in this sausage and vegetable soup. No need to make any side dishes; this is a definitive one-bowl meal.

---

1   POUND TURKEY ITALIAN SAUSAGE, CASINGS REMOVED

2   TEASPOONS OLIVE OIL

1   CUP CHOPPED ONION

3   CLOVES GARLIC, SLICED

5   CUPS LOW-SODIUM CHICKEN BROTH

1   28-OUNCE CAN CRUSHED TOMATOES, UNDRAINED

2   MEDIUM ZUCCHINI, TRIMMED, HALVED LENGTHWISE, AND SLICED

2   MEDIUM CARROTS, PEELED AND THINLY SLICED

1   MEDIUM RED BELL PEPPER, SEEDED AND CHOPPED

½   CUP DRY RED WINE

2   TABLESPOONS DRIED BASIL

2   TABLESPOONS DRIED OREGANO

1   10-OUNCE PACKAGE REFRIGERATED CHEESE TORTELLINI

OPTIONAL: FRESHLY GRATED PARMESAN CHEESE

Place the sausage in a large saucepan set over medium-high heat. Cook, breaking up the sausage using the back of a wooden spoon, about 10 minutes. Transfer the sausage to a paper-towel-lined plate to drain. Wipe the saucepan with a paper towel.

Heat the oil in the same saucepan over medium-high heat. Add the onion. Season with salt and pepper. Cook and stir 5 minutes. Add the garlic. Cook and stir 1 minute.

Add the broth, tomatoes with their juices, zucchini, carrots, bell pepper, wine, basil, and oregano. Bring to a boil. Reduce heat to medium low. Partially cover and simmer 20 minutes, until vegetables are tender.

Add the tortellini to the pan. Cook 8 to 9 minutes, until tender. Stir in sausage. Season with salt and pepper to taste. If desired, serve sprinkled with the Parmesan cheese. **Makes 8 servings.**

NUTRITION PER SERVING:
CALORIES 271; FAT 5.7G (SAT 2.1G, MONO 1.7G, POLY 0.6G);
PROTEIN 15G; CHOLESTEROL 23MG; SODIUM 562MG; CARBOHYDRATE 43.9G.

60 MINUTES

Rice Congee Soup (Jook)

Many Chinese begin their day with a warm bowl of congee, but it is also a rich and satisfying dinner. The word congee (also known as "jook" in the region of Canton) comes from the Indian "kanji," which refers to the water in which the rice has been boiled. Creamy, slightly salty, and thick like porridge, it is comfort food with a capital 'C.' Be sure to set out a variety of condiments for topping the soup exactly to your taste.

5½ CUPS WATER

4   CUPS LOW-SODIUM CHICKEN BROTH

1   CUP UNCOOKED JASMINE OR LONG GRAIN RICE

1   TEASPOON SALT

1   1-INCH PIECE PEELED FRESH GINGER, CUT INTO 4 SLICES

3   CUPS COOKED DICED OR SHREDDED COOKED CHICKEN (E.G., FROM A PURCHASED ROTISSERIE CHICKEN)

OPTIONAL GARNISHES: CHOPPED GREEN ONIONS, CHOPPED FRESH CILANTRO LEAVES, JULIENNE-CUT PEELED FRESH GINGER, LOW-SODIUM SOY SAUCE

Place the water, broth, rice, salt and ginger in a large pot set over medium-high heat. Bring to a boil. Continue boiling, uncovered, 15 minutes, stirring occasionally.

Reduce heat to medium low, cover, and cook 40 minutes longer, until the soup has a creamy consistency, stirring occasionally. Remove from heat and keep warm.

Discard ginger pieces. Stir the chicken into the soup. Serve garnished with the green onions, cilantro, julienne-cut ginger, and soy sauce, if desired. **Makes 6 servings.**

NUTRITION PER SERVING:
CALORIES 207; FAT 5.3G (SAT 1.5G, MONO 2.1G, POLY 1.3G);
PROTEIN 13.5G; CHOLESTEROL 33MG; SODIUM 609MG; CARBOHYDRATE 24.7G.

60 MINUTES

Chicken Posole

Posole (pronounced poh-SO-lay) is a traditional Latin American soup that has been served since pre-Columbian times. It continues to be especially popular in Mexico and the American Southwest, where it is often served at celebrations. Numerous variations on basic posole exist, and some Latin American restaurants actually specialize in offering only posole, much like noodle shops in Japan and China. The foundation of all posole is hominy or nixtamal, dried corn that has been treated with an alkali such as lime. If you're not familiar with hominy, it tastes like tender pieces of fresh corn tortillas (in other words, delicious). Cans of white and yellow hominy are inexpensive and readily available at supermarkets next to the canned corn.

1 TABLESPOON OLIVE OIL	2 15-OUNCE CANS WHITE HOMINY, DRAINED
1½ CUPS CHOPPED ONION	⅓ CUP CANNED TOMATO PASTE
4 CLOVES GARLIC, MINCED	3 CUPS SHREDDED COOKED CHICKEN (E.G.,
2 TABLESPOONS CHILI POWDER	FROM A PURCHASED ROTISSERIE CHICKEN)
1 TEASPOON DRIED OREGANO	2 TABLESPOONS FRESH LIME JUICE
1 TEASPOON GROUND CUMIN	1 CUP CHOPPED FRESH CILANTRO LEAVES
5 CUPS LOW-SODIUM CHICKEN BROTH	OPTIONAL GARNISHES: DICED AVOCADO,
1 14.5-OUNCE CAN PETITE DICED TOMATOES,	THINLY SLICED RADISHES, CRUMBLED
UNDRAINED	TORTILLA CHIPS

Heat the oil in a large saucepan over medium heat. Add the onion. Season with salt and pepper. Cook and stir 5 minutes. Add the garlic, chili powder, oregano, and cumin. Cook and stir 30 seconds.

Add the broth, tomatoes with their juices, hominy, and tomato paste to pan. Bring to a boil. Reduce heat to medium low, cover, and simmer 15 minutes.

Stir in the chicken and lime juice. Cook 2 minutes to heat through. Season with salt and pepper to taste. Stir in the cilantro. Serve plain or, if desired, with assorted garnishes as suggested. **Makes 6 servings.**

NUTRITION PER SERVING:
CALORIES 241; FAT 8.6G (SAT 2.7G, MONO 3.1G, POLY 1.4G);
PROTEIN 20.5G; CHOLESTEROL 62MG; SODIUM 952MG; CARBOHYDRATE 36.1G.

30 MINUTES

Tortilla Chicken Soup

A crumble of corn tortilla chips adds both body and crunch to this filling soup. The fresh cilantro and diced avocado on top add splashes of cool, vibrant flavor.

1 TEASPOON CANOLA OIL	1 CUP FROZEN CORN, UNTHAWED
2 CLOVES GARLIC, MINCED	1 10-OUNCE CAN DICED TOMATOES AND
1½ TABLESPOONS CHILI POWDER	GREEN CHILES, UNDRAINED
2 TEASPOONS GROUND CUMIN	1 TABLESPOON FRESH LIME JUICE
4 CUPS LOW-SODIUM CHICKEN BROTH	1 CUP BAKED TORTILLA CHIPS, CRUSHED
1½ CUPS CHOPPED COOKED CHICKEN BREAST	¼ CUP SHREDDED MONTEREY JACK CHEESE
(E.G., FROM A PURCHASED ROTISSERIE	¼ CUP CHOPPED FRESH CILANTRO LEAVES
CHICKEN)	½ CUP PEELED AND DICED AVOCADO

Heat the oil in a large saucepan set over medium-high heat. Add the garlic, chili powder, and cumin. Cook and stir 1 minute.

Add the broth, chicken, corn, and tomatoes with their juices. Bring to a boil. Reduce heat to medium low and simmer 5 minutes. Stir in the lime juice and season with salt and pepper to taste. Ladle into 4 bowls and top with equal amounts of Monterey Jack cheese, cilantro, and avocado. **Makes 4 servings.**

NUTRITION PER SERVING:
CALORIES 207; FAT 7.4G (SAT 2.4G, MONO 2.8G, POLY 1.2G);
PROTEIN 22.3G; CHOLESTEROL 51MG; SODIUM 604MG; CARBOHYDRATE 12.6G.

20 MINUTES

Chunky Turkey Vegetable Soup

WITH SWEET POTATOES & GREENS

A few fresh vegetables and some leftover turkey (or purchased turkey from the deli counter) is all you'll need to create this satisfying soup—perfect for cold nights and holiday nostalgia.

1   TABLESPOON OLIVE OIL

1¼ CUPS CHOPPED ONION

2   CLOVES GARLIC, MINCED

1   LARGE SWEET POTATO, PEELED, QUAR-
    TERED LENGTHWISE, AND THINLY SLICED

1   14.5-OUNCE CAN DICED TOMATOES,
    UNDRAINED

4   CUPS LOW-SODIUM CHICKEN BROTH

3   TABLESPOONS CANNED TOMATO PASTE

1   TABLESPOON CHOPPED FRESH ROSEMARY
    LEAVES OR 1½ TEASPOONS DRIED,
    CRUMBLED

2   CUPS DICED COOKED TURKEY BREAST

4   CUPS SLICED PREWASHED MUSTARD
    GREENS (OR ½ OF A 16-OUNCE BAG
    FROZEN MUSTARD GREENS)

Heat the oil in a large saucepan set over medium-high heat. Add the onion. Cook, stirring occasionally, until softened, about 5 minutes. Add the garlic. Cook and stir 1 minute.

Add the sweet potato, tomatoes with their juices, broth, tomato paste, and rosemary. Bring to a boil. Reduce the heat to medium low and simmer 15 to 20 minutes, until the sweet potato is tender.

Stir in the turkey and mustard greens. Cover and simmer 5 minutes. Season with salt and pepper to taste. **Makes 4 servings.**

NUTRITION PER SERVING:
CALORIES 234; FAT 7.2G (SAT 1.7G, MONO 3.1G, POLY 1.5G);
PROTEIN 16.1G; CHOLESTEROL 66MG; SODIUM 478MG; CARBOHYDRATE 32.4G.

45 MINUTES

Asian Chicken Noodle Soup

I became enamored of a spicy chicken noodle soup at a Vietnamese restaurant located a few blocks from my parents' home in the San Francisco Bay area. I would have to travel several hours to get something similar in my neck of the woods, so I put together my own take on the spicy concoction (with what I think are great results).

1	TABLESPOON CANOLA OIL		2	TABLESPOONS LOW-SODIUM SOY SAUCE
2	TABLESPOONS MINCED PEELED FRESH GINGER		1	TEASPOON TOASTED (DARK) SESAME OIL
2	CLOVES GARLIC, MINCED		1	TABLESPOON LIGHT BROWN SUGAR
2	SMALL RED CHILES, SEEDED AND FINELY CHOPPED, DIVIDED USE		6	OUNCES RICE STICK NOODLES
6	CUPS LOW-SODIUM CHICKEN BROTH, DIVIDED USE		1	BUNCH BABY BOK CHOY, TRIMMED AND CHOPPED
¾	POUND BONELESS, SKINLESS CHICKEN BREASTS, TRIMMED OF FAT		2	GREEN ONIONS, TRIMMED AND THINLY SLICED DIAGONALLY

Heat the oil in a large saucepan set over medium-high heat. Add the ginger, garlic, and half of the chiles. Cook and stir 30 seconds.

Add 2 cups of the broth. Cover. Bring to a boil. Reduce heat to medium low. Add the chicken. Cook for 5 minutes or until just cooked through. Using tongs, transfer the chicken to a cutting board. Slice crossways into strips.

Add the soy sauce, sesame oil, brown sugar, and the remaining 4 cups of the broth. Cover. Increase the heat to medium high. Bring to a boil. Add the noodles. Cook 6 minutes, until noodles are tender. Add the bok choy and cook 2 minutes longer, until bok choy is wilted. Season with salt and pepper to taste.

Serve the soup topped with the sliced chicken, green onions, and remaining chiles. **Makes 6 servings.**

NUTRITION PER SERVING:
CALORIES 238; FAT 7.5G (SAT 1.5G, MONO 3.1G, POLY 2.8G); PROTEIN 9.4G; CHOLESTEROL 49MG; SODIUM 507MG; CARBOHYDRATE 35G.

Gingered Chicken & Vegetable Soup

This aromatic soup is a balanced blend of peppery ginger broth, hearty chunks of chicken, and crisp-tender vegetables. It adds up to one big bowl of calm.

1 TABLESPOON CANOLA OIL	1 15-OUNCE CAN STRAW MUSHROOMS, DRAINED
¼ CUP PEELED MINCED FRESH GINGER	1 8-OUNCE CAN SLICED WATER CHESTNUTS, DRAINED
3 CLOVES GARLIC, MINCED	
1 SMALL RED ONION, THINLY SLICED	3 CUPS DICED OR SHREDDED COOKED CHICKEN BREAST (E.G., FROM A PURCHASED ROTISSERIE CHICKEN)
8 CUPS LOW-SODIUM CHICKEN BROTH	
2 MEDIUM CARROTS, PEELED AND THINLY SLICED	
2 CUPS FRESH OR FROZEN SNOW PEAS, ENDS TRIMMED	2 TEASPOONS FRESH LEMON JUICE

Heat the oil in a large saucepan set over medium heat. Add the ginger, garlic, and onion. Cook and stir 3 minutes.

Add the broth and carrots to the pan. Bring to a boil. Reduce heat to medium low, cover, and simmer 15 to 20 minutes, until the carrots are tender. Add the snow peas. Cook 5 minutes longer.

Add the mushrooms, water chestnuts, chicken, and lemon juice. Cook 2 minutes to heat through and blend flavors. Season with salt and pepper to taste. **Makes 8 servings.**

NUTRITION PER SERVING:
CALORIES 233; FAT 6.1G (SAT 3.1 G, MONO 1.6G, POLY 1.2G);
PROTEIN 16.1G; CHOLESTEROL 34MG; SODIUM 650MG; CARBOHYDRATE 35G.

30 MINUTES

West African Spicy Chicken & Peanut Soup

Tired of the same old chicken breasts for dinner? Try this spicy African soup for a delicious change of pace. The peanut butter adds substance and depth to the broth that is absolutely addictive.

1 POUND SKINLESS, BONELESS CHICKEN BREAST HALVES, CUT INTO 1-INCH PIECES	1½ TABLESPOONS CANOLA OIL
1 TABLESPOON HOT SAUCE	1½ CUPS CHOPPED ONION
1 TEASPOON GROUND CUMIN	2 MEDIUM ZUCCHINI, TRIMMED AND CUT INTO ½-INCH CUBES
4 CUPS LOW-SODIUM CHICKEN BROTH	2 TABLESPOONS ALL PURPOSE FLOUR
⅓ CUP CREAMY PEANUT BUTTER (DO NOT USE NATURAL OR OLD-FASHIONED)	1 CUP THICK-AND-CHUNKY-STYLE BOTTLED SALSA
2 TABLESPOONS TOMATO PASTE	

Place the chicken in a medium bowl and season with salt and pepper. Add hot sauce and cumin and toss to coat.

In another medium bowl whisk the broth, peanut butter, and tomato paste until smooth.

Heat the oil in a large saucepan set over medium-high heat. Add the onion and zucchini. Season with salt and pepper. Cook and stir 5 minutes. Add the chicken mixture. Cook and stir 3 to 4 minutes, until the chicken is no longer pink on the outside. Sprinkle with the flour. Cook and stir 1 minute.

Add the broth mixture and salsa to the saucepan. Cook 5 to 6 minutes, until the chicken is cooked through. Season with salt and pepper to taste. **Makes 4 servings.**

NUTRITION PER SERVING:
CALORIES 188; FAT 5.9G (SAT 1.3G, MONO 2.4G, POLY 1.6G);
PROTEIN 15.2G; CHOLESTEROL 21MG; SODIUM 456MG; CARBOHYDRATE 19.3G.

20 MINUTES

Country Captain Soup

Country Captain is a classic Southern chicken stew long associated with Georgia. Some food historians contend that it made its way to Savannah—once an important port in the spice trade—via a British sea captain traveling from India. Although I've adapted it from a thick stew to a soup, I've kept many of the other traditional elements in place, including tender chicken, onions, garlic, bell peppers, curry, cayenne, a little sweet from currants, and brightness from tomatoes.

1 TABLESPOON OLIVE OIL	1 28-OUNCE CAN DICED TOMATOES, UNDRAINED
2 CUPS CHOPPED ONION	
1 MEDIUM RED BELL PEPPER, SEEDED AND CHOPPED	1 LARGE GRANNY SMITH APPLE, PEELED AND COARSELY CHOPPED
4 GARLIC CLOVES, MINCED	5 CUPS LOW-SODIUM CHICKEN BROTH
1 POUND SKINLESS BONELESS CHICKEN BREAST HALVES, CUT INTO 1-INCH PIECES	¼ CUP ORZO (RICE-SHAPED PASTA) OR OTHER SMALL-SHAPED PASTA
1 TABLESPOON MILD CURRY POWDER	2 TABLESPOONS DRIED CURRANTS
2 TEASPOONS GRATED PEELED FRESH GINGER	½ CUP CHOPPED FRESH CILANTRO LEAVES
¼ TEASPOON CAYENNE PEPPER	OPTIONAL: PLAIN LOW-FAT OR NONFAT YOGURT FOR GARNISH

Heat the oil in a large saucepan set over medium-high heat. Add the onion, bell pepper, and garlic. Season with salt and pepper. Cook and stir 5 minutes. Add the chicken, curry powder, ginger, and cayenne. Cook and stir 2 minutes.

Add the tomatoes with their juices, apple, and broth to the pan. Bring to a boil. Reduce heat to medium low, cover, and simmer 20 minutes.

Stir the orzo and currants into the soup and simmer 7 to 8 minutes, until the orzo is just cooked through. Season with salt and pepper to taste. Ladle the soup into bowls. Top with the cilantro and garnish with a dollop of yogurt, if desired. **Makes 8 servings.**

NUTRITION PER SERVING:
CALORIES 236; FAT 4.8G (SAT 0.8G, MONO 1.1G, POLY 2.3G);
PROTEIN 18G; CHOLESTEROL 33MG; SODIUM 599MG; CARBOHYDRATE 31G.

45 MINUTES

Ajiaco (Potato, Corn, and Chicken Soup)

Ajiaco is a quintessential dish from Bogotá, Colombia. It's a great weekend soup, but it's also a celebration meal for the Bogotános who often make very large pots of it for festive occasions, such as Christmas. Cubed Yukon gold potatoes provide color, while grated russets gently release their starch to make the soup rich and thick without added cream. Be sure to use the small holes on a box grater for the russet potatoes to ensure that they will dissolve into the broth.

2 TEASPOONS CANOLA OIL	2 CUPS YUKON GOLD POTATO, PEELED AND CUT INTO CUBES
¾ CUP CHOPPED ONION	¼ CUP CHOPPED FRESH CILANTRO LEAVES
1 MEDIUM CARROT, PEELED AND THINLY SLICED (ABOUT ¾ CUP)	2 CUPS COOKED, SHREDDED CHICKEN BREAST (E.G., FROM A PURCHASED ROTIS-SERIE CHICKEN)
5 CUPS LOW-SODIUM CHICKEN BROTH	1 TABLESPOON FRESH LIME JUICE
1 CUP FROZEN CORN KERNELS	¾ TEASPOON HOT PEPPER SAUCE
1 TEASPOON DRIED OREGANO	
1 TEASPOON DRIED THYME LEAVES	
1¾ CUPS FINELY SHREDDED PEELED RUSSET POTATO	

Heat the oil in a large saucepan set over medium-high heat. Add the onion and carrot. Season with salt and pepper. Cook and stir 5 minutes.

Add the broth, corn, oregano, thyme, and russet potato. Bring to a boil. Reduce heat to medium, cover, and cook 20 minutes, stirring occasionally, until the potatoes are tender.

Add the Yukon gold potato. Cover and simmer 20 minutes, stirring frequently. Stir in the cilantro, chicken, lime juice, and hot sauce. Cook 2 minutes to heat through. Season with salt to taste. **Makes 6 servings.**

NUTRITION PER SERVING:
CALORIES 331; FAT 7.8G (SAT 1.7G, MONO 3.3G, POLY 1.6G);
PROTEIN 22.3G; CHOLESTEROL 47MG; SODIUM 434MG; CARBOHYDRATE 34.4G.

60 MINUTES

Chicken Chowder

WITH CHEDDAR CHEESE & BACON

Reminiscing about the cheddar cheese soups of my youth, I found myself wondering: Would a lighter version—lower in fat and calories—hold up? I put it to the test and am happy to report that the answer is a resounding "yes."

2 BACON SLICES, CHOPPED	2 CUPS AND DICED RED POTATOES
1 POUND BONELESS, SKINLESS CHICKEN BREASTS, CUT INTO 1-INCH PIECES	2 CUPS FROZEN WHOLE-KERNEL CORN
1 CUP CHOPPED ONION	½ CUP ALL-PURPOSE FLOUR
1 MEDIUM RED BELL PEPPER, SEEDED AND CHOPPED	2 CUPS 2% LOW-FAT MILK
2 CLOVES GARLIC, MINCED	1 CUP SHREDDED SHARP CHEDDAR CHEESE
5 CUPS LOW-SODIUM CHICKEN BROTH	1 TABLESPOON DIJON MUSTARD
	OPTIONAL: ¼ CUP CHOPPED CHIVES

Cook the bacon until crisp in a large saucepan set over medium-high heat until crisp. Remove the bacon from the pan with slotted spoon and drain on a paper-towel-lined plate.

Add the chicken, onion, bell pepper, and garlic to the bacon fat in the pan. Cook and stir 5 minutes. Add the broth and potatoes. Bring to a boil. Cover and reduce heat to medium low. Cook 20 minutes or until the potatoes are tender. Stir in the corn.

Place the flour in a medium bowl. Gradually add milk, stirring with a whisk until blended. Add the milk mixture to the soup. Cook and stir over medium heat 13 to 16 minutes, until thickened, stirring frequently. Stir in cheese and mustard. Cook 1 minute to melt the cheese. Season with salt and pepper to taste. Top with the bacon and garnish with the chives, if desired. **Makes 6 servings.**

NUTRITION PER SERVING:
CALORIES 306; FAT 7.5G (SAT 4.0G, MONO 2.2G, POLY 0.6G); PROTEIN 22.1G; CHOLESTEROL 31MG; SODIUM 376MG; CARBOHYDRATE 33.7G.

60 MINUTES

Turkey & Wild Rice Soup

I love wild rice—it tastes nutty with a slightly chewy texture—so it should be no surprise that this turkey soup is one of my favorites. Creamy and rich, you'll be hard-pressed to detect it is low-fat. Yum.

1 CUP UNCOOKED WILD RICE	2 TABLESPOONS SHERRY OR MARSALA
2 TEASPOONS OLIVE OIL	2 TEASPOONS DRY RUBBED SAGE
1 CUP CHOPPED ONION	½ TEASPOON FRESHLY GROUND BLACK PEPPER
2 CLOVES GARLIC, MINCED	1 8-OUNCE PACKAGE ⅓-LESS-FAT CREAM CHEESE, CUT INTO CUBES
3 CUPS LOW-SODIUM CHICKEN BROTH	2 CUPS DICED COOKED TURKEY BREAST
2 MEDIUM RUSSET POTATOES, CUT INTO ½-INCH PIECES	¼ CUP CHOPPED FRESH FLAT-LEAF PARSLEY LEAVES
3 CUPS 2% LOW-FAT MILK	
⅓ CUP ALL-PURPOSE FLOUR	

Cook the wild rice according to the package directions, omitting any salt and fat.

Meanwhile, heat the oil in a large saucepan set over medium-high heat. Add the onion. Season with salt and pepper. Cook and stir 5 minutes. Add the garlic. Cook and stir 1 minute.

Add the broth and potatoes. Bring to a boil. Cover and reduce heat to medium low. Cook 7 to 8 minutes, until the potatoes are tender.

In a medium bowl whisk the milk, flour, sherry, sage, and pepper until blended and smooth. Add the milk mixture to the pan. Cook and stir 5 minutes, until the soup thickens.

Reduce the heat to low. Add the cream cheese to the pan. Cook and stir 2 to 3 minutes, until the cream cheese is melted. Stir in the rice and turkey. Cook 1 minute to heat through. Season with salt and pepper to taste. Serve sprinkled with the parsley. **Makes 8 servings.**

NUTRITION PER SERVING:
CALORIES 280; FAT 7.1G (SAT 4.0G, MONO 1.1G, POLY 0.6G);
PROTEIN 24.4G; CHOLESTEROL 51MG; SODIUM 569MG; CARBOHYDRATE 28.2G.

60 MINUTES

Thai Chicken & Coconut Soup

Why resort to take-out? This spicy coconut broth, brimming with the flavors of Thailand, is a wonderful way to make weeknight chicken tempting again. To make the soup even more substantial, add about 2 cups of steamed jasmine rice or cooked rice noodles before serving.

2 TEASPOONS CANOLA OIL	1 TEASPOON GRATED LIME ZEST
1 POUND SKINLESS, BONELESS CHICKEN BREASTS, CUT INTO BITE-SIZED PIECES	1 TEASPOON SUGAR
3 TABLESPOONS MINCED PEELED FRESH GINGER	¼ CUP FRESH LIME JUICE
	2 TABLESPOONS THAI FISH SAUCE
1 TABLESPOON THAI GREEN CURRY PASTE	1 14-OUNCE CAN LIGHT COCONUT MILK
3 CUPS LOW-SODIUM CHICKEN BROTH	¼ CUP CHOPPED FRESH CILANTRO LEAVES
2 TEASPOONS GRATED LEMON ZEST	¼ CUP SLICED FRESH BASIL LEAVES

Heat the oil in a large saucepan set over medium-high heat. Add the chicken, ginger, and curry paste. Season with salt and pepper. Cook and stir 5 minutes.

Add the broth, lemon zest, lime zest, sugar, lime juice, and fish sauce. Bring to a boil. Reduce the heat to medium low. Cover and simmer 10 minutes.

Stir in the coconut milk. Cook 3 minutes. Season with salt and pepper to taste. Serve sprinkled with the cilantro and basil. **Makes 4 servings.**

NUTRITION PER SERVING:
CALORIES 228; FAT 5.2G (SAT 3.9G, MONO 0.7G, POLY 0.5G); PROTEIN 30.8G; CHOLESTEROL 75MG; SODIUM 478MG; CARBOHYDRATE 8.2G.

30 MINUTES

Chicken & Couscous Soup

WITH EXOTIC SPICES

If ever there was an easy, exotic dinner to brighten winter's gloom, this is it. The fresh mint and cilantro are musts, providing fresh contrast to the earthy whole wheat couscous and spicy broth.

1 TABLESPOON OLIVE OIL	½ CUP WHOLE WHEAT (OR REGULAR) COUSCOUS
1½ CUPS CHOPPED ONION	
2 TEASPOONS GROUND CUMIN	3 CUPS DICED OR SHREDDED COOKED CHICKEN (E.G., FROM A PURCHASED ROTISSERIE CHICKEN)
1½ TEASPOONS PAPRIKA	
1 TEASPOON GROUND CINNAMON	
½ TEASPOON GROUND TURMERIC	2 TEASPOONS FRESH LEMON JUICE
⅛ TEASPOON CAYENNE PEPPER	¼ CUP CHOPPED FRESH MINT LEAVES
7 CUPS LOW-SODIUM CHICKEN BROTH	¼ CUP CHOPPED FRESH CILANTRO LEAVES
2 TABLESPOONS CANNED TOMATO PASTE	
1 14.5-OUNCE CAN PETITE DICE TOMATOES, UNDRAINED	

Heat the oil in a large saucepan set over medium-high heat. Add the onion. Season with salt and pepper. Cook and stir 5 minutes. Add the cumin, paprika, cinnamon, turmeric, and cayenne. Cook and stir 1 minute.

Add the broth, tomato paste, and tomatoes with their juices. Bring to a boil. Stir the soup, and add the couscous. Reduce heat to low. Add the chicken. Cook, uncovered, 5 minutes, until the couscous is tender. Stir in the lemon juice, mint, and cilantro. Season with salt and pepper to taste. **Makes 8 servings.**

NUTRITION PER SERVING:
CALORIES 225; FAT 6.3G (SAT 1.2G, MONO 3.4G, POLY 1.1G);
PROTEIN 24.8G; CHOLESTEROL 60MG; SODIUM 355MG; CARBOHYDRATE 16.6G.

20 MINUTES

Golden Turkey Soup

WITH CORN & ORZO

Turkey, corn, and tender orzo pasta revel in a warm bath of golden broth, infused with a trio of exotic yet familiar spices: saffron, coriander, and cardamom.

1 TABLESPOON OLIVE OIL	½ CUP ORZO (RICE-SHAPED PASTA) OR OTHER SMALL-SHAPED PASTA
1½ CUPS CHOPPED ONION	3 CUPS FINELY DICED COOKED TURKEY BREAST
1 MEDIUM RED BELL PEPPER, SEEDED AND CHOPPED	1½ CUPS FROZEN CORN KERNELS, UNTHAWED
½ TEASPOON GROUND CORIANDER	⅓ CUP CHOPPED FRESH FLAT-LEAF PARSLEY LEAVES
¼ TEASPOON GROUND CARDAMOM	3 TABLESPOONS FRESH LEMON JUICE
1 LARGE PINCH SAFFRON THREADS	
8 CUPS LOW-SODIUM CHICKEN BROTH	

Heat the oil in a large saucepan set over medium-high heat. Add the onion and bell pepper. Season with salt and pepper. Cook and stir 5 minutes. Add the coriander and cardamom. Cook and stir 1 minute.

Add the saffron and broth. Bring to a boil. Add the pasta. Cook 7 to 8 minutes, until orzo is tender. Stir in the turkey, corn, and parsley. Cook 3 minutes to heat through. Stir in the lemon juice and season with salt and pepper to taste. **Makes 8 servings.**

NUTRITION PER SERVING:
CALORIES 228; FAT 6.3G (SAT 1.9G, MONO 2.2G, POLY 1.0G); PROTEIN 16.3G; CHOLESTEROL 242MG; SODIUM 541MG; CARBOHYDRATE 16.6G.

20 MINUTES

Chipotle Chicken Chowder

This warming southwestern soup is a welcome departure. Its spiciness is easily varied: just add more or less chipotles to suit your taste.

1 TABLESPOON OLIVE OIL	1½ POUNDS BONELESS, SKINLESS CHICKEN BREASTS
1½ WHOLE CHIPOTLE CHILES, CHOPPED (FROM A 7-OUNCE CAN)	2 15-OUNCE CANS HOMINY, DRAINED
1 16-OUNCE BAG FROZEN (THAWED) PEPPERS & ONIONS	1 12-OUNCE CAN FAT-FREE EVAPORATED MILK
1 CUP CHOPPED CARROT	1 14.5-OUNCE CAN CRUSHED TOMATOES, UNDRAINED
2 TEASPOONS GROUND CUMIN	⅓ CUP CHOPPED FRESH CILANTRO LEAVES
1 TEASPOON DRIED OREGANO	1 TABLESPOON FRESH LIME JUICE
6 GARLIC CLOVES, MINCED	
5 CUPS FAT-FREE, LESS-SODIUM CHICKEN BROTH	

Heat the oil in a large saucepan set over medium-high heat. Add the chiles, pepper and onion mixture, carrot, cumin, oregano, and garlic. Season with salt and pepper. Cook and stir 8 minutes.

Add the broth and bring to a boil. Add the chicken. Cover, reduce heat to medium low, and cook 20 minutes or until the chicken is cooked though. Remove the chicken with a slotted spoon. Cool slightly. Shred or chop the chicken.

Working in batches, purée the soup in a blender until smooth. Return the soup to the saucepan and reheat gently. Stir in the hominy, evaporated milk, tomatoes with their juices, and chicken. Cook over low heat 5 minutes to blend flavors. Stir in cilantro and lime juice and season with salt and pepper to taste. **Makes 8 servings.**

NUTRITION PER SERVING:
CALORIES 246; FAT 6.2G (SAT 2.3G, MONO 2.4G, POLY 0.8G);
PROTEIN 24.5G; CHOLESTEROL 60MG; SODIUM 472MG; CARBOHYDRATE 21.8G.

45 MINUTES

Turkey Curry Soup

Standard cream of turkey soup pales in the face of this rich and satisfying recipe, which features the flavors of India: aromatic ginger, curry powder, coconut, and lime.

1 TABLESPOON UNSALTED BUTTER

2½ CUPS CHOPPED ONION

2 TABLESPOONS MINCED PEELED FRESH GINGER

1½ TABLESPOONS MILD CURRY POWDER

3 CLOVES GARLIC, MINCED

1 CUP PEELED AND CHOPPED CARROTS

1 CUP CHOPPED CELERY

2 MEDIUM TART-SWEET APPLES, PEELED, CORED, AND CHOPPED, DIVIDED USE

8 CUPS LOW-SODIUM CHICKEN BROTH, DIVIDED USE

1¼ CUPS UNCOOKED LONG GRAIN RICE

3 CUPS SHREDDED COOKED TURKEY

2 TABLESPOONS FRESH LIME JUICE

1 14-OUNCE CAN LIGHT COCONUT MILK

½ CUP ALL-PURPOSE FLOUR

OPTIONAL: HOT SAUCE

⅓ CUP CHOPPED FRESH CILANTRO OR MINT LEAVES

⅓ CUP CHOPPED DRY-ROASTED PEANUTS OR CASHEWS

⅓ CUP FLAKED SWEETENED COCONUT, TOASTED

Melt the butter in a large saucepan set over medium-high heat. Add the onion. Season with salt and pepper. Cook and stir 5 minutes. Add the ginger, curry powder, and garlic. Cook and stir 1 minute.

Add the carrots, celery, half of the apples, and 4 cups of the broth. Bring to a boil. Reduce heat to medium low. Simmer 20 minutes.

While the soup simmers, prepare the rice according to package directions.

Working in batches, purée the soup in a blender until smooth. Return the soup to the saucepan and stir in the turkey, lime juice, the remaining broth, and cooked rice.

Whisk the coconut milk and flour in a medium bowl until blended and smooth. Add to the soup. Bring to a boil over medium-high heat. Reduce heat to medium low. Simmer 10 minutes, until thick, stirring constantly. Season with salt to taste and hot sauce, if desired. Serve topped with the cilantro, peanuts, and coconut. **Makes 8 servings.**

NUTRITION PER SERVING:
CALORIES 302; FAT 7.8G (SAT 3.2G, MONO 2.8G, POLY 2.1G);
PROTEIN 19.3G; CHOLESTEROL 36MG; SODIUM 523MG; CARBOHYDRATE 30.1G.

45 MINUTES

4. SEAFOOD

Soups

PESCI IN ACQUA PAZZA, SALMON **CHOWDER**, SEABASS IN SWEET & SOUR BROTH, GINGERED FISH & WATERCRESS **SOUP**, TUNISIAN AROMATIC FISH **SOUP**, SOUTHEAST ASIAN FISH **SOUP**, SPANISH SEAFOOD **SOUP**, BOUILLABAISSE, LATE SUMMER SEAFOOD **SOUP** WITH SMOKY LEMON ROUILLE, CIOPPINO, THAI HOT & SOUR **SOUP** WITH SHRIMP, GINGER & LIME, SHRIMP **BISQUE**, CRAB, TOMATO & BASIL **BISQUE**, CREAMY CLAM **CHOWDER**, COCONUT SHRIMP **SOUP**, SHRIMP & SCALLOP VERDE POSOLE, CHINESE SHRIMP & EGG DROP **SOUP**, ROASTED RED BELL PEPPER & PARMESAN **BISQUE** WITH SHRIMP, CORN & CRAB CHESAPEAKE **CHOWDER**, MANHATTAN CLAM **CHOWDER**, FISH-ERMAN'S **CHOWDER**, CAJUN-SPICED GUMBO **SOUP**, AND CARIBBEAN PEPPER POT

Pesci in Acqua Pazza

(WHITE FISH IN CRAZY WATER)

Sophisticated and healthy, yet incredibly easy, this soup brings the flavor of the Mediterranean to your table in minutes. The anchovy paste can be found in tubes in the section where canned tuna is shelved. It is a convenient and frugal way to add tremendous flavor to soups such as this.

1 POUND FRESH OR FROZEN (THAWED) HALIBUT OR OTHER WHITE-FLESH, SKINLESS FISH FILLETS, CUT INTO 1-INCH CHUNKS	½ CUP DRY WHITE WINE
1 TABLESPOON OLD BAY SEASONING	1 7-OUNCE JAR ROASTED RED BELL PEPPERS, DRAINED AND CHOPPED
1 TABLESPOON OLIVE OIL	3 TABLESPOONS CAPERS, DRAINED, COARSELY CHOPPED
1 TEASPOON CRUSHED RED PEPPER FLAKES	3 GREEN ONIONS, TRIMMED AND CHOPPED
3 CLOVES GARLIC, MINCED	4 CUPS LOW-SODIUM CHICKEN OR VEGETABLE BROTH
2 TEASPOONS ANCHOVY PASTE OR 2 TEA-SPOONS ASIAN FISH SAUCE (E.G., NAAM PLA)	1 CUP CHOPPED FRESH CILANTRO OR FLAT-LEAF PARSLEY LEAVES

Season the fish with salt and pepper and the Old Bay seasoning.

Heat the oil in a large saucepan over medium-high heat. Add the red pepper flakes, garlic, and anchovy paste. Cook and stir 30 seconds. Add the fish. Cook 3 minutes, stirring after the first 2 minutes. Add the wine. Cook and stir 2 minutes, scraping up any browned bits from the bottom of the pan.

Add the roasted peppers, capers, green onions, and broth. Bring to a simmer and cook 3 to 5 minutes longer to blend the flavors. Season with salt and pepper to taste. Serve sprinkled with ¼ cup of the cilantro or parsley. **Makes 4 servings.**

NUTRITION PER SERVING:
CALORIES 204; FAT 6.1G (SAT 1.1G, MONO 3.1G, POLY 1.6G);
PROTEIN 26G; CHOLESTEROL 44MG; SODIUM 429MG; CARBOHYDRATE 13G.

30 MINUTES

Salmon Chowder

Here is one of my go-to soups for easy dinners with company, specifically because it has a serious "wow" factor. Even though it involves some peeling and chopping, it's still fuss-free and assembled in no time. My one caution: Be careful when cooking the potatoes in the milk. Keep the heat relatively low or it will boil over.

3½ CUPS 1% LOW-FAT MILK

1 12-OUNCE CAN FAT-FREE EVAPORATED MILK

1 TABLESPOON UNSALTED BUTTER

1¼ CUPS CHOPPED ONION

2 TABLESPOONS ALL-PURPOSE FLOUR

1 POUND RED-SKIN POTATOES, PEELED AND DICED INTO ¼-INCH PIECES

1 POUND SKINLESS SALMON FILLET, CUT INTO 1-INCH CHUNKS

4 OUNCES SMOKED SALMON, FINELY CHOPPED

¼ CUP CHOPPED FRESH DILL

2 TABLESPOONS FRESH LEMON JUICE

Place the low-fat milk and evaporated milk in a medium saucepan set over medium heat. Heat until hot but not boiling.

Meanwhile, melt the butter in a large saucepan set over medium heat. Add the onion. Season with salt and pepper. Cook and stir 5 minutes. Mix in the flour. Cook and stir 2 minutes.

Increase heat to medium high. Add the potatoes and hot milk. Bring to a boil, whisking constantly to prevent scorching on bottom of pan. Reduce heat to medium low. Cook 10 to 12 minutes, until the potatoes are almost tender.

Add the salmon and cook 5 to 6 minutes, until slightly firm. Add the smoked salmon, dill, and lemon juice. Simmer 2 minutes to heat through and blend flavors. Season with salt and pepper to taste. **Makes 6 servings.**

NUTRITION PER SERVING:

CALORIES 311; FAT 7.7G (SAT 2.0G, MONO 3.3G, POLY 1.5G);

PROTEIN 21.6G; CHOLESTEROL 47MG; SODIUM 386MG; CARBOHYDRATE 39.1G.

30 MINUTES

Seabass in Sweet & Sour Broth

Seabass has a delicate flavor that is easily overpowered. Perhaps surprisingly, the extroverted combination of flavors in this sweet and sour broth doesn't mask the flavor of the fish, but rather adds complementary bright, savory flavors.

4 6-OUNCE FRESH OR FROZEN (THAWED) SKINLESS SEABASS (OR OTHER WHITE FISH, SUCH AS HALIBUT OR COD) FILLETS, (ABOUT 1-INCH THICK)	2½ TABLESPOONS UNSEASONED RICE VINEGAR
2 TABLESPOONS TAMARI OR LOW-SODIUM SOY SAUCE	1 2-INCH PIECE FRESH GINGER, PEELED AND CUT INTO THIN STRIPS
4 CUPS LOW-SODIUM CHICKEN OR VEGETABLE BROTH	½ TEASPOON HOT SAUCE
¼ CUP HONEY	OPTIONAL: HOT, COOKED BROWN OR JASMINE RICE
3 TABLESPOONS TOMATO PASTE	2 GREEN ONIONS, TRIMMED AND THINLY SLICED
	¼ CUP CHOPPED FRESH CILANTRO LEAVES

Place the fish fillets on a dinner plate. Drizzle the tamari over both sides of the fish. Cover and refrigerate while preparing the broth.

Place the broth, honey, tomato paste, vinegar, ginger, and hot sauce in a large saucepan set over medium-high heat. Bring to a boil. Reduce heat to low and cook 8 minutes.

Add the fish to the pan. Cover and cook 7 to 8 minutes, until the fish is slightly firm to the touch and the centers are almost opaque (the fish should not be fully cooked at this point). Turn off the heat. Cover and let sit 2 more minutes.

Divide the fish and broth evenly among 4 shallow bowls (if desired, fill bowls with hot, cooked rice first). Season with salt and pepper to taste. Sprinkle with the green onions and cilantro. **Makes 4 servings.**

Camilla's Note: To check the fish for doneness, make a small slit with a knife to check.

30 MINUTES

NUTRITION PER SERVING:
CALORIES 190; FAT 5.7G (SAT 1.2G, MONO 2.4G, POLY 1.5G);
PROTEIN 31.4G; CHOLESTEROL 70MG; SODIUM 116MG; CARBOHYDRATE 1.2G.

Gingered Fish & Watercress Soup

This soup draws me in every time. The clean assertiveness of watercress accentuates the fresh ginger and plays off the earthiness of the mushrooms and sesame oil. It tastes so sophisticated, and yet, beyond the fresh watercress, can be made with staples from the pantry and freezer.

½ OUNCE DRIED CHINESE BLACK MUSHROOMS
(OR DRIED SHIITAKE MUSHROOMS)

½ CUP BOILING WATER

1½ TEASPOONS CANOLA OIL

1 TEASPOON TOASTED (DARK) SESAME OIL

3 GREEN ONIONS, MINCED

2 CLOVES GARLIC, MINCED

2 TABLESPOONS MINCED PEELED FRESH
GINGER

3 CUPS LOW-SODIUM CHICKEN OR
VEGETABLE BROTH

1 8-OUNCE BOTTLE CLAM JUICE

1 TABLESPOON DRY SHERRY

1 TABLESPOON LOW-SODIUM SOY SAUCE

1 POUND FRESH OR FROZEN (THAWED)
WHITE-FLESH, SKINLESS FISH FILLETS, CUT
INTO 1-INCH CHUNKS (E.G., COD OR HAL-
IBUT)

1 LARGE BUNCH WATERCRESS, TOUGH STEMS
TRIMMED OFF

Soak the mushrooms in the boiling water until softened, about 20 minutes. Drain the mushrooms, reserving soaking the liquid. Squeeze out excess moisture. Thinly slice the caps, discarding the stems.

Meanwhile, heat the oil and sesame oil in a large saucepan set over medium heat. Add the green onions, garlic, and ginger. Cook and stir 3 minutes. Add the sliced mushrooms. Cook and stir 3 minutes.

Add the broth, mushroom soaking liquid, clam juice, sherry, and soy sauce. Bring to a boil. Stir in the fish and watercress and boil 2 to 3 minutes, until the fish is just cooked through. Season with additional soy to taste. **Makes 4 servings.**

NUTRITION PER SERVING:
CALORIES 201; FAT 5.9G (SAT 1.3G, MONO 3.2G, POLY 1.7G);
PROTEIN 28.1G; CHOLESTEROL 70MG; SODIUM 367MG; CARBOHYDRATE 3.2G.

30 MINUTES

Tunisian Aromatic Fish Soup

Why you'll make it: Because it's an exotic, spicy spin on simple fish soup, made better with an out-of-the-ordinary combination of herbs and spices. Frozen fish fillets make it extra easy and convenient to make on a harried weeknight.

1   TABLESPOON OLIVE OIL

1   TABLESPOON PAPRIKA

1½ TEASPOONS GROUND CUMIN

¼   TEASPOON CAYENNE PEPPER

3   CLOVES GARLIC, MINCED

6   CUPS LOW-SODIUM VEGETABLE BROTH

1   POUND YUKON GOLD POTATOES, PEELED
    AND DICED INTO ½-INCH PIECES

1   14.5-OUNCE CAN PETITE DICED TOMATOES,
    UNDRAINED

2   TABLESPOONS CHOPPED FRESH MINT
    LEAVES

1½ TABLESPOONS FRESH LEMON JUICE

⅓   CUP PLUS 1 TABLESPOON FINELY CHOPPED
    CILANTRO LEAVES

1   POUND FRESH OR FROZEN (THAWED)
    SKINLESS 1-INCH-THICK FIRM WHITE FISH
    FILLETS (E.G., COD OR HALIBUT)

Heat the oil in a large saucepan set over medium-high heat. Add the paprika, cumin, cayenne, and garlic. Cook and stir 1 minute.

Add the broth, potatoes, tomatoes with their juices, mint, lemon juice, and ⅓ cup of the cilantro. Bring to a boil. Reduce heat to medium low and cook, partially covered, 20 minutes. Uncover and cook 10 minutes longer, until the potatoes are very tender.

Add the fish and cook 10 minutes, until the fish is cooked through. Using the back of a spoon, break up fish into smaller pieces. Season the soup with salt and pepper to taste. Serve the soup with the remaining cilantro. **Makes 6 servings.**

NUTRITION PER SERVING:
CALORIES 235; FAT 8.1G (SAT 1.3G, MONO 5.4G, POLY 1.6G);
PROTEIN 25.1G; CHOLESTEROL 54MG; SODIUM 573MG; CARBOHYDRATE 20.2G.

60
MINUTES

Southeast Asian Fish Soup

I developed this soup after tasting a similar concoction at a favorite Thai restaurant. My interpretation brings together many of the characteristic, exotic flavors of Thailand and Vietnam, but with readily available ingredients from the supermarket.

3 CUPS WATER

3 8-OUNCE BOTTLES CLAM JUICE

4 GREEN ONIONS, THINLY SLICED, WHITE AND GREEN PARTS SEPARATED

2 TABLESPOONS PEELED, MINCED FRESH GINGER

2 TEASPOONS GRATED LEMON ZEST

1 CLOVE GARLIC, MINCED

1 TEASPOON ASIAN CHILI PASTE (E.G., SAMBAL OELEK)

1 TABLESPOON ASIAN FISH SAUCE (E.G., NAAM PLA)

1 POUND FRESH OR FROZEN (THAWED) SKINLESS 1-INCH-THICK FIRM WHITE FISH FILLETS (E.G., COD OR HALIBUT), CUT INTO ¾-INCH CUBES

¼ POUND BUTTON MUSHROOMS, TRIMMED AND SLICED

2 LARGE CARROTS, PEELED AND GRATED

1 CUP FRESH CILANTRO LEAVES, COARSELY CHOPPED

1 TABLESPOON FRESH LIME JUICE

Place the water, clam juice, white portion of the green onions, ginger, lemon zest, garlic, and chili paste in a large saucepan set over medium-high heat. Bring to a boil. Reduce the heat to medium low, cover, and simmer 10 minutes. Stir in the fish sauce.

Add the fish, mushrooms, and carrots to the pan. Cover, increase heat to medium, and cook 4 to 5 minutes, until the fish is cooked through. Stir in the cilantro, green portions of the green onions, and lime juice. Season with salt and pepper to taste. **Makes 6 servings.**

NUTRITION PER SERVING:
CALORIES 143; FAT 3.1G (SAT 0.5G, MONO 1.8G, POLY 0.5G);
PROTEIN 15.7G; CHOLESTEROL 33MG; SODIUM 380MG; CARBOHYDRATE 14.6G.

30 MINUTES

Spanish Seafood Soup

Seafood soup recipes are diverse and plentiful in Spain, all taking advantage of local ingredients and regional herbs and spices. This is my own interpretation, a heady, fragrant slurry thick with fish, clams, and sausage, and seasoned with a trio of familiar Spanish flavors: orange, oregano, and hot smoked paprika. Complement it with plenty of crusty French bread.

2 TEASPOONS OLIVE OIL	1 7-OUNCE JAR ROASTED RED BELL PEPPERS, DRAINED AND COARSELY CHOPPED
½ OF A 16-OUNCE PACKAGE LIGHT SMOKED SAUSAGE, DICED	3 8-OUNCE BOTTLES CLAM JUICE
1½ TEASPOONS GRATED ORANGE ZEST	1 POUND FRESH OR FROZEN (THAWED) WHITE-FLESH, SKINLESS FISH FILLETS, CUT INTO 1-INCH CHUNKS
1¼ TEASPOONS DRIED OREGANO	1 6.5-OUNCE CAN CHOPPED CLAMS
1 TEASPOON HOT SMOKED PAPRIKA (PIMENTÓN)	
½ CUP DRY WHITE WINE	
1 28-OUNCE CAN CRUSHED TOMATOES, UNDRAINED	

Heat the oil in a large saucepan set over medium-high heat. Add the sausage. Cook and stir 3 minutes. Add the orange zest, oregano, paprika, and white wine. Bring to a boil. Cook until the liquid is almost evaporated.

Add the tomatoes with their juices, red bell peppers, and clam juice to the pan. Bring to a boil. Add the fish and clams. Reduce heat to low, cover, and cook 10 minutes. Season with salt and pepper to taste. **Makes 6 servings.**

NUTRITION PER SERVING:
CALORIES 221; FAT 4.1G (SAT 0.6G, MONO 2.3G, POLY 0.6G);
PROTEIN 20.5G; CHOLESTEROL 42MG; SODIUM 345MG; CARBOHYDRATE 26.4G.

30 MINUTES

Bouillabaisse

This is a much simplified version of the most famous fish stew of the Mediterranean. Its home is considered to be Marseilles, although it is made in every little port throughout the coastal regions of Provence. If desired, serve it topped with a dollop of smoky lemon rouille (see page 103) in additional to the toasted bread.

1 LARGE PINCH SAFFRON	3 CUPS LOW-SODIUM VEGETABLE BROTH
2 TABLESPOONS FRESH ORANGE JUICE	½ POUND FRESH OR FROZEN (THAWED)
1½ TABLESPOONS OLIVE OIL	WHITE-FLESH, SKINLESS FISH FILLETS, CUT
2 CLOVES GARLIC, MINCED	INTO 1-INCH CHUNKS
1 LARGE ONION, PEELED AND SLICED	½ POUND FRESH OR FROZEN (THAWED)
1 MEDIUM FENNEL BULB, TRIMMED AND	MEDIUM SHRIMP, PEELED AND DEVEINED
THINLY SLICED	6 OUNCES FRESH OR CANNED LUMP
1 TEASPOON GRATED ORANGE ZEST	CRABMEAT
1 14.5-OUNCE CAN DICED TOMATOES,	1 BUNCH FLAT-LEAF PARSLEY LEAVES,
UNDRAINED	CHOPPED
3 8-OUNCE BOTTLES CLAM JUICE	OPTIONAL: 6 SLICES TOASTED CRUSTY BREAD

Combine the saffron and orange juice in a small cup. Let stand 10 minutes.

Meanwhile, heat the oil in a large saucepan set over medium-high heat. Add the garlic, onion, and fennel. Season with salt and pepper. Cook and stir 8 minutes. Add the saffron mixture, orange zest, tomatoes with their juices, clam juice, and broth. Bring to a boil. Cook, uncovered, 20 minutes.

Reduce the heat to medium. Add the fish. Cook 2 minutes. Add the shrimp. Cook 2 minutes more. Add the crabmeat. Cook 2 minutes longer, until the fish flakes easily. Season with salt and pepper to taste.

Serve sprinkled with the parsley and topped with the crusty bread, if desired. **Makes 6 servings.**

NUTRITION PER SERVING:
CALORIES 253; FAT 6.8G (SAT 1.1G, MONO 1.4G, POLY 3.0G);
PROTEIN 29.5G; CHOLESTEROL 126MG; SODIUM 706MG; CARBOHYDRATE 19.8 G.

60 MINUTES

Late Summer Seafood Soup

WITH SMOKY LEMON ROUILLE

Inspired by summer produce and seafood, this brightly spiced soup will transport you to sunny shores.

2 TEASPOONS OLIVE OIL	1 LARGE PINCH SAFFRON
4 CLOVES GARLIC, MINCED, DIVIDED USE	½ POUND FRESH OR FROZEN (THAWED)
1 28-OUNCE CAN CRUSHED TOMATOES,	WHITE-FLESH, SKINLESS FISH FILLETS, CUT
UNDRAINED	INTO 1-INCH CHUNKS (E.G., COD OR
1 CUP DRY WHITE WINE	HALIBUT)
¼ CUP REDUCED-FAT MAYONNAISE	½ POUND FRESH OR FROZEN (THAWED)
1 TEASPOON SWEET SMOKED PAPRIKA	MEDIUM SHRIMP, SHELLED, DEVEINED,
(PIMENTÓN)	AND CUT INTO ½-INCH PIECES
2 TABLESPOONS FRESH LEMON JUICE	2 CUPS FRESH OR FROZEN (UNTHAWED)
2 CUPS LOW-SODIUM CHICKEN OR	CORN KERNELS
VEGETABLE BROTH	⅓ CUP SLICED FRESH BASIL LEAVES

Heat the oil in a large saucepan set over medium heat. Add all but ½ teaspoon of the garlic. Cook and stir 30 seconds. Add the tomatoes with their juices and wine. Increase the heat to medium high. Bring to a boil. Cook and stir 15 minutes.

Meanwhile, make the rouille by whisking the mayonnaise, paprika, lemon juice, and the remaining ½ teaspoon garlic in a small bowl. Season with salt and pepper.

Add the broth and saffron to the tomato mixture. Cook 5 minutes. Add the fish and shrimp. Cook 3 to 5 minutes, until the fish and shrimp are opaque. Add the corn. Cook 1 minute longer (2 to 3 minutes if using frozen corn). Season with salt and pepper to taste. Serve drizzled with the rouille and sprinkled with the basil. **Makes 4 servings.**

45 MINUTES

NUTRITION PER SERVING:
CALORIES 226; FAT 7.1G (SAT 1.1G, MONO 4.6G, POLY 1.2G);
PROTEIN 6.3G; CHOLESTEROL 56MG; SODIUM 502MG; CARBOHYDRATE 37.2G.

Cioppino

According to legend, Portuguese and Italian immigrants (many of them fisherman) in the San Francisco Bay are responsible for creating cioppino (pronounced chuh-PEE-noh). This is my interpretation of the seafood and tomato-based classic, made new with fresh fennel and a light, streamlined prep.

1 MEDIUM FENNEL BULB, TRIMMED AND VERY COARSELY CHOPPED (RESERVE FENNEL FRONDS)	1 28-OUNCE CAN CRUSHED TOMATOES, UNDRAINED
1 MEDIUM ONION, TRIMMED AND QUARTERED	1½ CUPS FULL-BODIED RED WINE (E.G., ZINFANDEL OR PINOT NOIR)
3 CLOVES GARLIC, PEELED	2 8-OUNCE BOTTLES CLAM JUICE
1 TABLESPOON OLIVE OIL	1 POUND FRESH OR FROZEN (THAWED) WHITE-FLESH, SKINLESS FISH FILLETS, CUT INTO 2-INCH CHUNKS (E.G., COD OR HALIBUT)
2 BAY LEAVES	
1½ TEASPOONS DRIED THYME	
1½ TEASPOONS SALT	
1 TEASPOON FRESHLY CRACKED BLACK PEPPER	1 POUND CULTIVATED MUSSELS, DEBEARDED

Place the fennel, onion, and garlic in a food processor. Process until coarsely chopped.

Heat the oil in a large saucepan or Dutch oven set over medium-high heat. Add the chopped vegetables, bay leaves, thyme, salt, and pepper. Cook and stir 4 minutes.

Add the tomatoes with their juices, wine, and clam juice. Bring to a boil. Reduce heat to medium low and simmer, covered, 20 minutes.

Stir in the fish and mussels and cook, uncovered, 5 to 6 minutes, until the fish is just cooked through and the mussels open wide. Remove the bay leaves. Season with salt and pepper to taste. Mince the reserved fennel fronds. Serve the soup sprinkled with the fennel fronds. **Makes 6 servings.**

Camilla's Note: Discard any mussels that remain unopened after 6 minutes.

NUTRITION PER SERVING:
CALORIES 268; FAT 6.7G (SAT 1.8G, MONO 4.1G, POLY 0.6G);
PROTEIN 28.7G; CHOLESTEROL 54MG; SODIUM 594MG; CARBOHYDRATE 14.8G.

45 MINUTES

Thai Hot & Sour Soup

WITH SHRIMP, GINGER & LIME

Thai red curry paste adds so much to the ready-made broth in this recipe. If you don't like Indian curry, try Thai curry anyway; it is quite different from the former. It comes in small jars and can be found in the Asian food section of the grocery store, or you can order it from Thai Kitchen, Taste of Thai, or amazon.com. The curry pastes keep in the refrigerator for several months.

1 TABLESPOON CANOLA OIL	1 POUND FRESH OR FROZEN (THAWED)
1½ TABLESPOONS BOTTLED THAI RED CURRY	MEDIUM SHRIMP, PEELED, DEVEINED, AND
PASTE	HALVED LENGTHWISE
5¼ CUPS LOW-SODIUM CHICKEN BROTH	4 OUNCES SHIITAKE (OR WHITE) MUSH-
2 TEASPOONS FINELY GRATED LIME ZEST	ROOMS, STEMMED AND SLICED THIN
3 TABLESPOONS MINCED PEELED FRESH	4 CUPS NAPA CABBAGE, CUT CROSSWISE
GINGER	INTO ⅛-INCH-THICK SLICES
3 TABLESPOONS FRESH LIME JUICE	⅓ CUP CHOPPED FRESH CILANTRO LEAVES
1 TABLESPOON ASIAN FISH SAUCE (E.G.,	2 GREEN ONIONS, TRIMMED AND THINLY
NAAM PLA)	SLICED
1½ TEASPOONS SUGAR	OPTIONAL: THINLY SLICED RED CHILES
2 TABLESPOONS CORNSTARCH	

Heat the oil in heavy, large saucepan set over medium heat. Add the curry paste and stir until it begins to stick to the pan, about 4 minutes. Stir in the broth, lime zest, and ginger. Bring to a boil. Reduce the heat to medium and simmer 5 minutes.

In a small bowl whisk the lime juice, fish sauce, sugar, and cornstarch until blended.

Add the shrimp, mushrooms, and lime juice mixture to the pan. Cook until the shrimp begin to turn pink, about 3 minutes. Stir in the cabbage. Cook 1 minute until the cabbage begins to wilt. Season with salt and pepper to taste. Serve the soup sprinkled with the cilantro, green onions, and chiles, if desired. **Makes 6 servings.**

30 MINUTES

NUTRITION PER SERVING:
CALORIES 143; FAT 3.7G (SAT 0.4G, POLY 1.2G, MONO 1.5G);
PROTEIN 19.9G; CHOLESTEROL 122.8MG; SODIUM 687MG; CARBOHYDRATE 6.8G.

Shrimp Bisque

A fresh green salad and a crusty baguette are natural complements to this chic and easy soup.

1	TABLESPOON UNSALTED BUTTER	¼	CUP CANNED TOMATO PASTE
1¼	CUPS CHOPPED ONION	3	TABLESPOONS BRANDY (OR COGNAC)
3	8-OUNCE BOTTLES CLAM JUICE	1	TEASPOON GRATED ORANGE ZEST
⅓	CUP LONG GRAIN WHITE RICE	⅛	TEASPOON CAYENNE PEPPER
1	POUND FRESH OR FROZEN (THAWED)	1	12-OUNCE CAN FAT-FREE EVAPORATED
	MEDIUM SHRIMP, PEELED AND DEVEINED		MILK

Melt the butter in a large saucepan set over medium heat. Add the onion. Cook and stir 5 minutes. Add the clam juice and rice. Bring to a boil. Reduce the heat to low, cover, and simmer until the rice is tender, about 20 minutes.

Add the shrimp to the pan. Cover and simmer 1 minute. Set aside 8 shrimp for garnish.

Working in batches, purée the soup in a blender until smooth. Return the soup to the saucepan and reheat gently. Whisk in the tomato paste, brandy, orange zest, and cayenne. Gradually whisk in the evaporated milk. Bring the soup to a simmer. Season with salt and pepper to taste.

Serve the soup garnished with the reserved shrimp and an additional sprinkle of cayenne, if desired. **Makes 4 servings.**

NUTRITION PER SERVING:
CALORIES 201; FAT 6.7G (SAT 3.2G, MONO 1.7G, POLY 1.2G);
PROTEIN 19.9G; CHOLESTEROL 133MG; SODIUM 380MG; CARBOHYDRATE 15.2G.

45 MINUTES

Crab, Tomato & Basil Bisque

Buttery and lush with chunks of fresh crab, this soup, though simple to prepare, tastes indulgent.

1 TABLESPOON UNSALTED BUTTER	⅓ CUP ALL PURPOSE FLOUR
2 SMALL ROMA TOMATOES, SEEDED AND CHOPPED	2½ CUPS CLAM-TOMATO JUICE (E.G., CLAM-ATO)
⅓ CUP PLUS 3 TABLESPOONS CHOPPED FRESH BASIL LEAVES, DIVIDED USE	1 CUP CANNED FAT-FREE EVAPORATED MILK (FROM A 12-OUNCE CAN)
2 CLOVES GARLIC, MINCED	2 TEASPOONS OLD BAY SEASONING
10 OUNCES FRESH LUMP CRABMEAT, DIVIDED USE	¼ TEASPOON HOT PEPPER SAUCE
	2 TABLESPOONS FRESH LEMON JUICE

Melt the butter in heavy, large saucepan over medium-high heat. Add the tomatoes, ⅓ cup basil, garlic, and three-fourths of the crabmeat. Cook and stir 3 minutes. Whisk in the flour. Cook and stir 2 minutes.

Whisk in the clam-tomato juice, evaporated milk, Old Bay seasoning, and hot pepper sauce. Reduce the heat to low. Cook, stirring occasionally, until slightly thickened, about 10 minutes. Cool the soup slightly.

Working in batches, purée the soup in a blender until smooth. Return the soup to the saucepan and reheat gently. Stir in the lemon juice and season with salt and pepper to taste. Serve the soup topped with the remaining crabmeat and the remaining basil. **Makes 4 servings.**

NUTRITION PER SERVING:
CALORIES 169; FAT 5.3G (SAT 2.4G, MONO 1.9G, POLY 0.7G);
PROTEIN 10.8G; CHOLESTEROL 34MG; SODIUM 536MG; CARBOHYDRATE 18G.

20 MINUTES

Creamy Clam Chowder

This New England standard will always be the perfect thing for a chilly evening. Serve it with dark beer and crusty bread or oyster crackers; you don't need anything beyond that. When adding the chopped clams to the pot, try not to heat them for too long, or they will toughen.

3	SLICES BACON, CHOPPED	1	TEASPOON DRIED THYME
2	CUPS CHOPPED ONION	1	12-OUNCE CAN FAT-FREE EVAPORATED MILK
1	CUP CHOPPED CELERY	¼	TEASPOON FRESHLY GROUND BLACK PEPPER
4	CUPS RED BLISS POTATOES (ABOUT 1¼ POUNDS), DICED INTO ½-INCH PIECES	2	15-OUNCE CANS CHOPPED CLAMS
2	8-OUNCE BOTTLES CLAM JUICE		OPTIONAL: CHOPPED CHIVES

Cook the bacon in a large saucepan set over medium-high heat. Transfer the bacon with a slotted spoon to paper-towel-lined plate. Discard all but 1 tablespoon bacon fat. Add the onions and celery to the pan. Season with salt and pepper. Cook and stir 6 minutes.

Add the potatoes, clam juice, and thyme. Bring to a boil. Reduce heat to medium low, cover, and cook 25 to 30 minutes, until the potatoes are very tender. Season with salt and pepper again.

Transfer about 1 cup of the soup (mostly solids) to a blender. Purée until smooth. Return the purée to the pan. Add the evaporated milk, pepper, and clams. Reduce the heat to low. Simmer 5 minutes to blend flavors. Season with salt and pepper to taste. Serve sprinkled with the bacon and chives, if desired. **Makes 6 servings.**

NUTRITION PER SERVING:
CALORIES 187; FAT 5.2G (SAT 2.6G, MONO 1.8G, POLY 0.4G);
PROTEIN 11.8G; CHOLESTEROL 32MG; SODIUM 639MG; CARBOHYDRATE 23.7G.

60
MINUTES

Coconut Shrimp Soup

Coconut milk, ginger, and lime give this speedy soup undercurrents of tropical flavor. And though the flavors are light and fresh, it's a filling one-bowl meal thanks to plenty of shrimp and noodles in every serving.

1	TABLESPOON CANOLA OIL	3	CUPS LOW-SODIUM VEGETABLE BROTH
2	TABLESPOONS GRATED PEELED FRESH GINGER	1	TABLESPOON CORNSTARCH
2	CLOVES GARLIC, MINCED	2	TABLESPOONS WATER
1	TEASPOON GRATED LIME ZEST	8	OUNCES ANGEL HAIR PASTA
½	TEASPOON RED PEPPER FLAKES	1	POUND FRESH OR FROZEN (THAWED) MEDIUM SHRIMP, PEELED AND DEVEINED
6	MEDIUM CARROTS, PEELED, HALVED LENGTHWISE, AND THINLY SLICED	¼	CUP FRESH LIME JUICE
2¼	CUPS LIGHT COCONUT MILK (FROM 2 13.5-OUNCE CANS)	4	GREEN ONIONS, TRIMMED AND THINLY SLICED
		½	CUP SLICED FRESH BASIL LEAVES

Heat the oil in a large saucepan set over medium heat. Add the ginger, garlic, lime zest, and red pepper flakes. Cook and stir 1 minute. Add the carrots, coconut milk, and broth. In a small bowl, mix the cornstarch and water until smooth. Add to the pan. Bring to a boil. Cook 4 minutes.

Break the pasta in half and add to the pan. Return to a boil and reduce heat to medium. Cook, uncovered, 4 to 5 minutes, until the pasta is al dente and the carrots are just tender.

Add the shrimp to the pan. Cook 1 to 2 minutes, until opaque. Remove the pan from the heat. Stir in the lime juice and season with salt to taste. Serve topped with the green onions and basil. **Makes 6 servings.**

NUTRITION PER SERVING:
CALORIES 194; FAT 5.3G (SAT 3.3G, MONO 0.4G, POLY 0.9G);
PROTEIN 26.9G; CHOLESTEROL 172MG; SODIUM 778MG; CARBOHYDRATE 9.9G.

30 MINUTES

Shrimp & Scallop Verde Posole

Loaded with plump shrimp and scallops, this spicy seafood rendition of the southwestern hominy classic is a crowd-pleaser.

1 TABLESPOON OLIVE OIL	2 TABLESPOONS FINELY CHOPPED SUN-DRIED TOMATOES PACKED IN OIL
1 CUP CHOPPED ONION	
3 CLOVES GARLIC, MINCED	1 TABLESPOON FINELY GRATED LIME ZEST
¾ TEASPOON GROUND CUMIN	¾ POUND FRESH OR FROZEN (THAWED) MEDIUM SHRIMP, PEELED AND DEVEINED
3 8-OUNCE BOTTLES CLAM JUICE	
1 15-OUNCE CAN WHITE HOMINY, RINSED AND DRAINED	½ POUND FRESH OR FROZEN (THAWED) LARGE SEA SCALLOPS, HALVED HORIZONTALLY
1½ CUPS JARRED TOMATILLO SALSA (SALSA VERDE)	2 TEASPOONS FRESH LIME JUICE
	6 TABLESPOONS CHOPPED CILANTRO LEAVES, DIVIDED USE

Heat the oil in large saucepan set over medium-high heat. Add the onion and season with salt and pepper. Cook and stir 5 minutes. Add the garlic and cumin. Cook and stir 30 seconds.

Add the clam juice, hominy, salsa, sun-dried tomatoes, and lime zest. Cook, partially covered, 5 minutes.

Add the shrimp, scallops, and 3 tablespoons of the cilantro, adding small amounts of water to thin if necessary. Simmer 3 to 4 minutes, until the seafood is just opaque in the center. Stir in the lime juice. Season with salt and pepper to taste. Serve sprinkled with the remaining cilantro. **Makes 6 servings.**

NUTRITION PER SERVING:
CALORIES 163; FAT 6.1G (SAT 4.5G, MONO 1.0G, POLY 0.3G);
PROTEIN 18.1G; CHOLESTEROL 84MG; SODIUM 379MG; CARBOHYDRATE 10.4G.

20 MINUTES

Chinese Shrimp & Egg Drop Soup

Egg drop soup, also known as egg flower soup, is one of the easiest (and most inexpensive) soups you can make. The trick for making it excellent is how you handle the eggs. Here is what I advise: Lightly beat the egg so that no bubbles form and turn off the heat before pouring in the egg (this produces silkier threads). Pour the egg in a very slow stream, stirring—in one direction only—as soon as you start pouring in the egg.

5 CUPS LOW-SODIUM VEGETABLE BROTH	2½ TEASPOONS CORNSTARCH
1½ TEASPOONS LOW-SODIUM SOY SAUCE	1 6-OUNCE CAN SMALL SHRIMP, DRAINED
1 2-INCH PIECE FRESH GINGER, THINLY SLICED	2 LARGE EGGS, LIGHTLY BEATEN
1 CLOVE GARLIC, PEELED AND SMASHED	2 GREEN ONIONS, TRIMMED AND THINLY SLICED
2 TABLESPOONS DRY SHERRY	1½ TEASPOONS TOASTED (DARK) SESAME OIL

Place the broth, soy sauce, ginger, and garlic in a heavy, large saucepan and bring to a boil. Remove ginger and garlic with a slotted spoon and discard.

Mix the sherry and cornstarch in a small cup until blended. Add to the pan. Bring to a boil then reduce heat and simmer 2 minutes, until slightly thickened. Add the shrimp and season with salt and pepper to taste. Remove the pan from the heat.

Stir the eggs with a fork in a glass measuring cup. Pour the eggs into a medium-size zip-top plastic bag. Close the bag. Begin to stir the soup in a circular motion. Snip one very small corner from the plastic bag, then drizzle the eggs in a slow, steady stream into the soup. Simmer, undisturbed, until strands of the egg are cooked, about 1 minute.

Remove the pan from the heat and stir in the green onions and sesame oil. Season with additional soy sauce to taste. **Makes 4 servings.**

NUTRITION PER SERVING:
CALORIES 94; FAT 3.8G (SAT 1.1G, MONO 1.4G, POLY 0.6G);
PROTEIN 6.9G; CHOLESTEROL 110MG; SODIUM 335MG; CARBOHYDRATE 6.2G.

20 MINUTES

Roasted Red Bell Pepper & Parmesan Bisque

WITH SHRIMP

Though quick and easy, this soup flirts with extravagance: sautéed shrimp and a smooth purée of red peppers laced with Parmesan and paprika. The fresh basil garnish adds a striking color contrast as well as subtle notes of lemon, anise, clove, and camphor.

2	7-OUNCE JARS ROASTED RED BELL PEPPERS, DRAINED	¾	CUP CANNED FAT-FREE EVAPORATED MILK (FROM A 12-OUNCE CAN)
3½	CUPS LOW-SODIUM CHICKEN OR VEGETABLE BROTH, DIVIDED USE	½	CUP FRESHLY GRATED PARMESAN CHEESE
1½	TEASPOONS PAPRIKA	1	TABLESPOON OLIVE OIL
1	TEASPOON SUGAR	¾	POUND FRESH OR FROZEN (THAWED) LARGE SHRIMP, PEELED, DEVEINED AND COARSELY CHOPPED
½	TEASPOON HOT PEPPER SAUCE	¼	CUP THINLY SLICED FRESH BASIL

Cut 1 of the roasted peppers into matchstick-size strips and set aside.

Working in batches, purée the peppers and 1 cup of the broth in a blender until smooth. Place in a large saucepan. Whisk in the remaining broth and the paprika, sugar, and hot sauce. Simmer over low heat 7 to 8 minutes to blend flavors. Whisk in the evaporated milk and Parmesan cheese. Season with salt and pepper to taste.

Heat the oil in a medium skillet set over medium-high heat. Add the reserved bell pepper strips and shrimp. Cook and stir 3 minutes, until the shrimp are opaque. Season with salt and pepper to taste. Divide the shrimp mixture among 4 bowls.

Ladle the warm soup around the shrimp mixture. Sprinkle the basil over the soup and serve. **Makes 4 servings.**

NUTRITION PER SERVING:
CALORIES 168; FAT 4.3G (SAT 1.6G, MONO 1.1G, POLY 1.5G);
PROTEIN 15.6G; CHOLESTEROL 145MG; SODIUM 472MG; CARBOHYDRATE 13.6G.

20 MINUTES

Corn & Crab Chesapeake Chowder

My Dad grew up near the Chesapeake Bay on the Eastern shore of Maryland, so when this soup got his "thumbs up," I knew I had a winner. Light, yet filling, it showcases some of summer's best flavors.

2 CUPS FRESH CORN KERNELS OR FROZEN (THAWED) PETITE WHITE CORN, DIVIDED USE

1½ CUPS 1% LOW-FAT MILK

2 GREEN ONIONS, TRIMMED AND SLICED, DIVIDED USE

1 8-OUNCE BOTTLE CLAM JUICE

2 TEASPOONS OLD BAY SEASONING

4 TEASPOONS FRESH LEMON JUICE, DIVIDED

1 TABLESPOON UNSALTED BUTTER

1 CUP DICED LEAN HAM

6 OUNCES FRESH OR CANNED LUMP CRAB-MEAT

Reserve ½ cup of the corn. Place the remaining corn and milk in a large saucepan set over medium-high heat. Bring to a boil. Remove from the heat and add half of the green onions. Cover and let stand 10 minutes. Transfer the mixture to a blender and purée until almost smooth.

Return the purée to the saucepan. Add the clam juice, Old Bay Seasoning, and 2 teaspoons lemon juice. Bring to a simmer over medium heat. Season with salt and pepper.

Melt the butter in a small skillet over medium heat. Add the ham and reserved ½ cup corn. Cook and stir 2 minutes. Add the crab, remaining 2 teaspoons of the lemon juice, and the remaining green onions. Cook and stir 2 minutes.

Stir the crab mixture into the corn mixture. Cook 2 minutes to blend flavors. Season with salt and pepper to taste. **Makes 4 servings.**

NUTRITION PER SERVING:
CALORIES 220; FAT 3.8G (SAT 0.6G, MONO 2.1G, POLY 0.8G);
PROTEIN 7.5G; CHOLESTEROL 41MG; SODIUM 452MG; CARBOHYDRATE 31.1G.

30 MINUTES

Manhattan Clam Chowder

Unlike creamy New England chowder, Manhattan clam chowder (also known as Fulton Fish Market clam chowder) has clear broth, plus tomato for color and flavor. According to Alton Brown, the addition of tomatoes in place of milk was initially the work of Portuguese immigrants in Rhode Island, as tomato-based stews were already a traditional part of Portuguese cuisine. Dubbing it "Manhattan" chowder was a pejorative, not complimentary, name given by scornful New Englanders to further distinguish the two types.

2 BACON SLICES, CUT INTO ½-INCH SQUARES	1¼ TEASPOONS DRIED THYME LEAVES
1½ CUPS CHOPPED ONION	½ TEASPOON RED PEPPER FLAKES
1 LARGE GREEN BELL PEPPER, SEEDED AND DICED SMALL	3 8-OUNCE BOTTLES CLAM JUICE
¾ CUP FINELY CHOPPED CELERY	2 14.5-OUNCE CAN PETITE DICE TOMATOES, UNDRAINED
1 POUND NEW POTATOES, DICED INTO ¼-INCH PIECES (ABOUT 2 CUPS)	¼ CUP CANNED TOMATO PASTE
4 CLOVES GARLIC, MINCED	2 15-OUNCE CANS CHOPPED CLAMS
	½ CUP CHOPPED FRESH FLAT-LEAF PARSLEY LEAVES

Cook the bacon in a large saucepan set over medium-high heat 5 minutes, until crisp. Use a slotted spoon to transfer the bacon to a paper-towel-lined plate. Discard all but 1 tablespoon fat from pan. Add the onion, green pepper, and celery. Season with salt and pepper. Cook and stir 5 minutes.

Add the potatoes, garlic, thyme, red pepper, clam juice, tomatoes with their juices, and tomato paste. Bring to a boil. Reduce heat to medium low, cover, and simmer 10 minutes.

Stir in the clams. Cook, covered, 5 minutes, stirring occasionally, to blend flavors. Stir in parsley and bacon. Season with salt and pepper to taste. **Makes 6 servings.**

NUTRITION PER SERVING:
CALORIES 143; FAT 3.1G (SAT 0.5G, MONO 1.9G, POLY 0.5G); PROTEIN 8.1G; CHOLESTEROL 21MG; SODIUM 451MG; CARBOHYDRATE 21.8G.

30 MINUTES

Fisherman's Chowder

Whether they feature shellfish, smoked fish, or fresh fish, chowders are quintessential New England cooking. Mine is prepared with a mixture of shrimp, scallops, and crabmeat. Cayenne adds a touch of heat and bacon, a bit of smokiness.

2 BACON SLICES, FINELY CHOPPED	½ POUND FRESH OR FROZEN (THAWED) SEA SCALLOPS, QUARTERED AND TOUGH MUSCLE REMOVED
2 LARGE SHALLOTS, FINELY CHOPPED	
1 POUND NEW POTATOES, DICED INTO ¼-INCH PIECES	½ POUND FRESH OR CANNED LUMP CRABMEAT
1 8-OUNCE BOTTLE CLAM JUICE	3 TABLESPOONS CHOPPED FRESH CILANTRO LEAVES, DIVIDED USE
2½ CUPS 2% LOW-FAT MILK	
⅛ TEASPOON CAYENNE PEPPER	3 TABLESPOONS CHOPPED FRESH CHIVES, DIVIDED USE
⅓ POUND FRESH OR FROZEN (THAWED) MEDIUM SHRIMP, SHELLED, DEVEINED, AND CUT INTO ½-INCH PIECES	

Cook the bacon in a large saucepan set over medium-high heat 5 minutes, until crisp. Use a slotted spoon to transfer the bacon to a paper-towel-lined plate. Discard all but 1 tablespoon fat from pan. Add the shallots. Season with salt and pepper. Cook and stir 5 minutes.

Add the potatoes and clam juice. Cover and cook 8 minutes, until the potatoes are tender and most of the liquid has evaporated. Stir in the milk and cayenne and heat just to a simmer.

Stir in the shrimp and scallops. Reduce heat to medium low and cook 3 to 5 minutes, stirring occasionally, until the shellfish is just cooked through. Stir in the crabmeat and half of the cilantro and chives. Cook 1 minute. Season with salt and pepper to taste. Serve topped with the bacon and remaining cilantro and chives. **Makes 4 servings.**

30 MINUTES

NUTRITION PER SERVING:
CALORIES 307; FAT 8.1G (SAT 3.5G, MONO 3.1G, POLY 0.9G);
PROTEIN 24.4G; CHOLESTEROL 57MG; SODIUM 611MG; CARBOHYDRATE 33.9G.

Cajun-Spiced Gumbo Soup

Gumbo is a stew or soup that originated in Louisiana and is popular across the Gulf Coast of the United States as well as the South. It is made from a flavorful broth—shellfish, meat, or poultry—a thickener (such as filé powder or okra), and the vegetable "holy trinity": celery, bell peppers, and onion. The soup is traditionally served over rice, but to keep the preparation and cleanup streamlined, I add the rice directly to the saucepan.

1½ TABLESPOONS CANOLA OIL

2 TABLESPOONS ALL-PURPOSE FLOUR

1¼ CUPS CHOPPED ONION

1 MEDIUM GREEN BELL PEPPER, SEEDED AND CHOPPED

¾ CUP CHOPPED CELERY

5 CUPS LOW-SODIUM CHICKEN OR VEGETABLE BROTH

¾ CUP UNCOOKED LONG GRAIN WHITE RICE

1 14.5-OUNCE CAN DICED TOMATOES, UNDRAINED

2 TEASPOONS DRIED THYME LEAVES

2 TEASPOONS HOT SAUCE

½ POUND FRESH OR FROZEN (THAWED) MEDIUM SHRIMP, SHELLED AND DEVEINED

6 OUNCES FRESH OR CANNED LUMP CRABMEAT

2 GREEN ONIONS, TRIMMED AND CHOPPED

Heat the oil in a large saucepan set over medium-high heat. Add the flour. Cook and stir 4 minutes, until the mixture is medium brown. Add the onion, bell pepper, and celery. Season with salt and pepper. Cook and stir 5 minutes.

Whisk the broth into the pan. Bring to a boil. Add the rice and reduce heat to low. Cook, covered, 15 to 20 minutes, until the rice is just tender.

Add the tomatoes with their juices, thyme, and hot sauce. Cook 5 minutes. Add the shrimp. Cook 4 to 5 minutes, until opaque. Add the crabmeat. Cook 1 minute to heat through. Season with salt and pepper to taste. Serve sprinkled with the green onions. **Makes 6 servings.**

NUTRITION PER SERVING:

CALORIES 222; FAT 6.1G (SAT 1.7G, MONO 1.2G, POLY 3.1G); PROTEIN 11.2G; CHOLESTEROL 145MG; SODIUM 459MG; CARBOHYDRATE 20.4G.

45 MINUTES

Caribbean Pepper Pot

Also called callaloo, this Jamaican dish has many guises and can be made with meats as well as fish and seafood. It dates back to the Arawak Indians, who prepared a stew that was kept going on the fire with the addition of new ingredients every day. I've kept this version simple with shrimp and a short cooking time.

1   TABLESPOON CANOLA OIL

1½ CUPS CHOPPED ONION

3   CLOVES GARLIC, MINCED

5   CUPS LOW-SODIUM CHICKEN OR
    VEGETABLE BROTH

1   14.5-OUNCE CAN DICED TOMATOES,
    UNDRAINED

1   LARGE SWEET POTATO, PEELED AND DICED
    INTO ½-INCH PIECES

1½ CUPS FROZEN SLICED OKRA, UNTHAWED

2   BAY LEAVES

1   TABLESPOON HOT SAUCE (MORE OR LESS
    TO TASTE)

1   TEASPOON GROUND ALLSPICE

¾   TEASPOON DRIED THYME

½   OF A 16-OUNCE BAG FROZEN CHOPPED
    KALE OR COLLARD GREENS, UNTHAWED

1   CUP CANNED LIGHT COCONUT MILK (FROM
    A 14-OUNCE CAN)

¾   POUND FRESH OR FROZEN (THAWED)
    MEDIUM SHRIMP, SHELLED AND DEVEINED

Heat the oil in a large saucepan set over medium-high heat. Add the onion. Season with salt and pepper. Cook and stir 5 minutes. Add the garlic. Cook and stir 1 minute.

Add the broth, tomatoes with their juices, sweet potato, okra, bay leaves, hot sauce, allspice, thyme, and greens. Bring to a boil. Reduce the heat to medium low, partially cover, and cook 25 minutes, until the sweet potatoes are tender.

Stir in the coconut milk and the shrimp. Simmer 3 to 5 minutes, until the shrimp are just opaque. Season with salt and pepper to taste. **Makes 8 servings.**

NUTRITION PER SERVING:
CALORIES 238; FAT 3.0G (SAT 1.7G, MONO 0.5G, POLY 0.7G);
PROTEIN 9.1G; CHOLESTEROL 59MG; SODIUM 391MG; CARBOHYDRATE 37G.

60 MINUTES

5. MEAT

Soups

Stuffed Green Pepper Soup, Mexican Meatball Soup, Italian Wedding Soup, Holishkes (Stuffed Cabbage) Soup, Lasagna Soup, Mongolian Hot Pot Soup, Pho Bo (Spicy Beef Vietnamese Noodle Soup), Smoky Chili-Beef Soup, Middle Eastern Beef & Bulgur Soup with Aromatic Spices, Asian Beef Noodle Soup with Cinnamon & Anise, Beef & Snow Pea Soup, Japanese Udon Beef Soup, Enlightened Scotch Broth, Lamb, Spinach & Couscous Soup, Portuguese Sausage, Sweet Potato & Spinach Soup, Garlic Soup with Poached Eggs & Ham, Sausage and Kale Soup, Shanghai Seared Pork & Noodle Soup, Rustic Sausage Soup with Pasta & Beans, Puerto Rican Ham Soup with Pigeon Peas & Sofrito, Swedish Yellow Split Pea Soup with Ham & Fresh Dill, and Cassoulet Soup

Stuffed Green Pepper Soup

I've recast the ingredients from my mother's recipe for stuffed green peppers (one of my childhood favorites) in an extra-easy, weeknight soup. I could eat this once a week, every week.

½	POUND EXTRA-LEAN GROUND BEEF	2	CUPS LOW-SODIUM BEEF BROTH
2	MEDIUM GREEN BELL PEPPERS, SEEDED AND CHOPPED	1	CUP WATER
1	MEDIUM RED BELL PEPPER, SEEDED AND CHOPPED	¾	CUP UNCOOKED WHITE RICE
		1	14.5-OUNCE CAN DICED TOMATOES, UNDRAINED
1	CUP CHOPPED ONION	1½	CUPS GOOD-QUALITY BOTTLED MARINARA SAUCE
2	TEASPOONS DRIED BASIL		

Cook the beef in a large saucepan set over medium-high heat, breaking up any chunks with the back of a wooden spoon, 4 minutes or until the beef is no longer pink.

Add the bell peppers and onion. Season with salt and pepper. Cook and stir 5 minutes. Stir in the basil, broth, water, and rice. Bring to a boil. Reduce heat, cover, and simmer 20 to 25 minutes, until the rice is tender.

Stir in the tomatoes with their juices and marinara sauce. Simmer 5 minutes to blend flavors. Season with salt and pepper to taste. **Makes 6 servings.**

NUTRITION PER SERVING:
CALORIES 219; FAT 7.2G (SAT 2.6G, MONO 2.9G, POLY 0.8G);
PROTEIN 11.7G; CHOLESTEROL 25MG; SODIUM 422MG; CARBOHYDRATE 27.5G.

45 MINUTES

Mexican Meatball Soup

Ready-made meatballs add quick and delicious heft, while chili powder, cumin, and oregano enrich store-bought broth for a quick and truly delicious south-of-the-border meal in a bowl.

1	TABLESPOON CANOLA OIL	8	CUPS LOW-SODIUM CHICKEN BROTH, DIVIDED USE
2	CUPS CHOPPED ONION	½	CUP ALL-PURPOSE FLOUR
4	CLOVES GARLIC, MINCED	20	FROZEN (THAWED) PRECOOKED MEAT-BALLS, HALVED
3	TABLESPOONS CHILI POWDER		
2	TEASPOONS GROUND CUMIN	½	CUP CHOPPED CILANTRO LEAVES
1	TEASPOON DRIED OREGANO	3	TABLESPOONS FRESH LIME JUICE
2	4-OUNCE CANS DICED GREEN CHILES		OPTIONAL GARNISHES: CHOPPED CILANTRO LEAVES, CRUSHED BAKED TORTILLA CHIPS, DICED AVOCADO
1	28-OUNCE CAN DICED TOMATOES, UNDRAINED		
2	TEASPOONS HOT SAUCE		

Heat the oil in a large saucepan set over medium-high heat. Add the onion. Season with salt and pepper. Cook and stir 5 minutes. Add the garlic, chili powder, cumin, and oregano. Cook and stir 1 minute.

Add the chiles, tomatoes with their juices, hot sauce, and 7 cups of the broth. Bring to a boil, then reduce heat to medium low and simmer 10 minutes.

In a small bowl whisk the flour and the remaining 1 cup broth until smooth. Whisk into the soup. Increase heat to high and bring to a boil. Reduce heat to medium low and simmer 5 minutes.

Add the meatballs and simmer an additional 5 minutes. Stir in the cilantro and lime juice, then season with salt and pepper to taste. If desired, serve soup with suggested garnishes. **Makes 8 servings.**

NUTRITION PER SERVING:
CALORIES 297; FAT 9.3G (SAT 2.6G, MONO 4.1G, POLY 1.5G);
PROTEIN 24.9G; CHOLESTEROL 52MG; SODIUM 501MG; CARBOHYDRATE 29.8G.

45 MINUTES

Italian Wedding Soup

This soup is delicate but filling at the same time with its pasta and baby meatballs. Unless you have some teenage football players in the house, this is a main-dish soup.

1 SMALL ONION, GRATED	3 LARGE EGGS, DIVIDED USE
⅓ CUP CHOPPED FRESH ITALIAN PARSLEY LEAVES	½ POUND EXTRA-LEAN GROUND BEEF
	½ POUND GROUND PORK
2 CLOVES GARLIC, MINCED	12 CUPS LOW-SODIUM CHICKEN BROTH
1 TEASPOON SALT	1¼ CUPS DITALINI OR OTHER VERY SMALL-
¼ CUP PLAIN BREADCRUMBS	SHAPED PASTA
6 TABLESPOONS FRESHLY GRATED PARME-SAN CHEESE, DIVIDED USE	1 POUND CURLY ENDIVE, TRIMMED AND COARSELY CHOPPED

In a large bowl combine the grated onion, parsley, garlic, salt, breadcrumbs, 4 tablespoons of the Parmesan cheese, and 1 egg until blended. Add the beef and pork and mix until just blended.

Shape the meat mixture into 1-inch-diameter meatballs (about 1½ teaspoons per ball). Place on a cookie sheet.

Place the broth in a large saucepan set over high heat. Bring to a boil. Add the pasta and cook 5 minutes. Reduce the heat to medium-high and add the meatballs and curly endive. Simmer, uncovered, 8 minutes longer, until the pasta and endive are tender and the meatballs are cooked through.

In a medium bowl whisk the remaining 2 eggs and the remaining Parmesan cheese. Stir the soup in a circular motion. Gradually drizzle the egg mixture into the broth, stirring gently with a fork to form thin stands of egg, about 1 minute. Season with salt and pepper to taste. **Makes 8 servings.**

NUTRITION PER SERVING:
CALORIES 263; FAT 8.3G (SAT 3.9G, MONO 3.1G, POLY 1.0G);
PROTEIN 26.1G; CHOLESTEROL 89MG; SODIUM 642MG; CARBOHYDRATE 25.8G.

30 MINUTES

Holishkes (Stuffed Cabbage) Soup

Holishkes are stuffed cabbage rolls served on Succoth, a joyous seven-day autumn harvest festival (a kind of Jewish Thanksgiving). The stuffing serves as a symbol of abundance. Here I've transformed the beloved, celebratory dish into a rich and robust soup. The result is every bit as festive.

8 CUPS LOW-SODIUM CHICKEN BROTH, DIVIDED USE	½ POUND EXTRA-LEAN GROUND BEEF
1 CUP UNCOOKED WHITE RICE	½ POUND GROUND PORK
1 TABLESPOON OLIVE OIL	¾ HEAD SAVOY CABBAGE, TRIMMED AND THINLY SLICED
1½ CUPS CHOPPED ONION	1 28-OUNCE CAN DICED TOMATOES, UNDRAINED
2 LARGE CARROTS, PEELED AND CHOPPED	1 6-OUNCE CAN TOMATO PASTE
2 CLOVES GARLIC, MINCED	⅓ CUP CHOPPED FLAT-LEAF PARSLEY LEAVES
2 TEASPOONS SMOKED PAPRIKA (PIMENTÓN)	1 TABLESPOON DRIED DILL
½ TEASPOON GROUND CINNAMON	
½ TEASPOON GROUND ALLSPICE	

Place 2 cups of the broth in a medium saucepan set over high heat. Bring to a boil, then add the rice. Reduce heat to low, cover, and simmer 18 to 20 minutes or until the rice is tender.

Meanwhile, heat the oil in a large saucepan set over medium-high heat. Add the onion and carrots. Season with salt and pepper. Cook and stir 5 minutes. Add the garlic, paprika, cinnamon, and allspice. Cook and stir 1 minute.

Add the beef and pork. Season with salt and pepper. Cook 5 to 6 minutes, breaking up with the back of a spoon, until the meat is no longer pink. Add the cabbage. Cook and stir 3 to 4 minutes, until the cabbage is slightly wilted.

Add the tomatoes with their juices, tomato paste, and the remaining 6 cups broth. Increase the heat to high and bring to a boil. Reduce the heat to low and simmer 5 minutes. Stir in the cooked rice, parsley, and dill. Season with salt and pepper to taste. **Makes 6 servings.**

NUTRITION PER SERVING:
CALORIES 282; FAT 7.6G (SAT 1.6G, MONO 3.7G, POLY 1.7G);
PROTEIN 26.6G; CHOLESTEROL 68MG; SODIUM 791MG; CARBOHYDRATE 30.1G.

45 MINUTES

Lasagna Soup

This speedy, soup-style version of the long-cooked classic is light but still substantial enough for a weeknight supper.

1	POUND EXTRA-LEAN GROUND BEEF	1	CUP MAFALDA OR CAMPENELLI PASTA
2	CUPS CHOPPED ONION	1	5-OUNCE BAG PREWASHED BABY SPINACH,
2	MEDIUM CARROTS, PEELED AND CHOPPED		COARSELY CHOPPED
1	12-OUNCE PACKAGE SLICED MUSHROOMS	1½	CUPS FAT-FREE RICOTTA CHEESE
4	CLOVES GARLIC, MINCED	½	CUP SLICED FRESH BASIL
4	CUPS LOW-SODIUM CHICKEN BROTH	¼	CUP FRESHLY GRATED PARMESAN CHEESE
1	26-OUNCE JAR GOOD-QUALITY MARINARA SAUCE		

Place the beef in a large saucepan set over medium-high heat. Season with salt and pepper. Cook 5 to 6 minutes, breaking up the beef with the back of a spoon, until it is no longer pink. Add the onion, carrots, mushrooms, and garlic. Season with salt and pepper. Cook and stir 8 minutes.

Add the broth and marinara sauce. Bring to a boil. Add the pasta and cook 10 to 12 minutes, until the pasta is tender. Stir in the spinach. Cook 3 minutes longer. Season with salt and pepper to taste.

Place ¼ cup ricotta cheese into each of 6 soup bowls. Ladle the soup over the ricotta cheese and sprinkle with the basil and Parmesan cheese. **Makes 6 servings.**

NUTRITION PER SERVING:
CALORIES 254; FAT 6.5G (SAT 3.5G, MONO 2.1G, POLY 0.3G);
PROTEIN 24.6G; CHOLESTEROL 69MG; SODIUM 560MG; CARBOHYDRATE 27.6G.

30 MINUTES

Mongolian Hot Pot Soup

This fragrant soup is brimming with both flavor and lean protein, perfect for chilly weather. The noodles, Japanese soba, are long, thin, and light brown in color thanks to their primary ingredient, buckwheat flour. If they are unavailable in your area, whole grain spaghetti is a fine substitute.

½ POUND EXTRA-LEAN GROUND BEEF

3 TABLESPOONS GRATED PEELED FRESH GINGER

2 TABLESPOONS LOW-SODIUM SOY SAUCE

1½ TEASPOONS TOASTED (DARK) SESAME OIL

¼ TEASPOON CAYENNE PEPPER

2 CLOVES GARLIC, MINCED

1 MEDIUM BUNCH BOK CHOY, TRIMMED, WASHED, AND THINLY SLICED

1 CUP THINLY SLICED SHIITAKE OR BUTTON MUSHROOMS

1 LARGE CARROT, PEELED AND DICED

3 GREEN ONIONS, THINLY SLICED

2 CUPS BOILING WATER

2 TABLESPOONS HOISIN SAUCE

4 CUPS LOW-SODIUM BEEF BROTH

4 OUNCES UNCOOKED SOBA (BUCKWHEAT) NOODLES

1 TABLESPOON RICE VINEGAR

Cook the beef in a large saucepan set over medium-high heat, breaking up any chunks with the back of a wooden spoon, 4 minutes or until the beef is no longer pink. Add the ginger, soy sauce, sesame oil, cayenne, and garlic. Cook and stir 1 minute longer.

Add the bok choy, mushrooms, carrot, and green onions to pan. Cook and stir 2 minutes or until the bok choy begins to wilt.

Add the water, hoisin, and broth to the pan. Bring to a boil, then stir in the noodles. Reduce the heat to low and simmer 5 minutes or until the noodles are tender. Season with salt and pepper to taste. **Makes 6 servings.**

NUTRITION PER SERVING:
CALORIES 197; FAT 5.6G (SAT 1.9G, MONO 2.2G, POLY 0.7G);
PROTEIN 13.4G; CHOLESTEROL 47MG; SODIUM 433MG; CARBOHYDRATE 24.2G.

30 MINUTES

Pho Bo

(SPICY BEEF VIETNAMESE NOODLE SOUP)

In Vietnam, people are fiercely loyal to their favorite version of pho bo. After a taste of this quicker, lighter version, I think you'll start to feel that same sense of loyalty. You can easily convert this from beef to chicken noodle soup by substituting 8 ounces of boneless, skinless chicken breast for the beef and chicken broth in place of the beef broth; made with chicken, it is known as pho ga.

¼ CUP COARSELY CHOPPED FRESH GINGER	2 TABLESPOONS FRESH LIME JUICE
2 WHOLE STAR ANISE	2 CUPS FRESH BEAN SPROUTS, RINSED AND DRAINED
1 CINNAMON STICK	
6 CUPS LOW-SODIUM BEEF BROTH	½ CUP MINCED GREEN ONIONS
½ POUND PIECE BONELESS BEEF SIRLOIN, TRIMMED OF ANY FAT	¼ CUP FRESH CILANTRO LEAVES, COARSELY CHOPPED
3 OUNCES DRIED FLAT RICE NOODLES	½ CUP FRESH BASIL LEAVES, SLICED
¼ CUP ASIAN FISH SAUCE (E.G., NAAM PLA)	SRIRACHA (SOUTHEAST ASIAN HOT SAUCE)
¼ TEASPOON CAYENNE	LIME WEDGES FOR GARNISH

Tie the ginger, star anise, and cinnamon in a piece of cheesecloth. Place in a large saucepan with the broth and bring to a boil. Reduce heat and simmer 15 minutes.

Meanwhile, cut the sirloin across the grain into very thin slices (use a very sharp knife).

In a large bowl soak the noodles in hot water to cover 15 minutes or until softened and pliable. While noodles are soaking, bring a kettle of salted water to a boil. Drain the noodles and cook in the boiling water, stirring 45 seconds, or until tender. Drain the noodles.

Remove cheesecloth of spices from the broth. Bring broth back to a boil. Stir in the fish sauce, cayenne, and lime juice. Add the sirloin and cook 30 to 45 seconds or until the sirloin changes color. Skim any froth from the soup. Season with salt and pepper to taste.

To serve, divide noodles into 4 bowls. Ladle the soup over the noodles. Sprinkle the sprouts, green onions, cilantro, and basil over the soup and serve with the Sriracha and lime wedges. **Makes 4 servings.**

NUTRITION PER SERVING:
CALORIES 222; FAT 4.9G (SAT 2.0G, MONO 1.9G, POLY 0.2G);
PROTEIN 23.5G; CHOLESTEROL 50.43MG; SODIUM 597MG; CARBOHYDRATE 19.6G.

45 MINUTES

Smoky Chili-Beef Soup

Chili from a can pales beside this 20-minute stovetop version. I've made this one closer to the consistency of soup for a change of pace. Canned refried beans and dark beer are the secrets to making it taste like it's cooked for hours rather than minutes.

½ POUND EXTRA-LEAN GROUND BEEF	2 15-OUNCE CANS LIGHT RED KIDNEY
3 TABLESPOONS CHILI POWDER	BEANS, UNDRAINED
1 TABLESPOON GROUND CUMIN	2 10-OUNCE CANS DICED TOMATOES WITH
1 TEASPOON CHIPOTLE CHILE POWDER	GREEN CHILES (E.G., RO-TEL), UNDRAINED
3 CUPS LOW-SODIUM BEEF BROTH	2 TABLESPOONS FRESH LIME JUICE
1 12-OUNCE BOTTLE DARK BEER	OPTIONAL GARNISHES: CHUNKY-STYLE SALSA,
1 15-OUNCE CAN FAT-FREE REFRIED BEANS	CUBED AVOCADO, FRESH CILANTRO LEAVES

Cook the beef in a large saucepan set over medium-high heat, breaking up any chunks with the back of a wooden spoon, 4 minutes or until the beef is no longer pink. Season with salt and pepper, then add the chili powder, cumin, and chipotle chile powder. Cook and stir 1 minute.

Add the broth, beer, refried beans, kidney beans, and tomatoes with their juices to the pan. Bring to a boil. Reduce heat to low, cover, and cook 10 to 12 minutes to blend flavors.

Stir in the lime juice and season with salt and pepper to taste. If desired, top servings with the salsa, avocado, or cilantro. **Makes 8 servings.**

NUTRITION PER SERVING:
CALORIES 261; FAT 5.7G (SAT 2.1G, MONO 2.1G, POLY 0.2G); PROTEIN 18.3G; CHOLESTEROL 30MG;
SODIUM 499MG; CARBOHYDRATE 30.3G.

20 MINUTES

Middle Eastern Beef & Bulgur Soup

WITH AROMATIC SPICES

With its notes of cumin, cinnamon, and coriander playing off the gentle heat of black pepper, this Middle Eastern soup combines the best parts of meaty kefta and vegetarian beans and grains. Its rich body makes it a seriously satisfying dinner any night of the week.

½ POUND EXTRA-LEAN GROUND BEEF

1½ CUPS CHOPPED ONION

2   CLOVES GARLIC, MINCED

1½ TEASPOONS GROUND CUMIN

1¼ TEASPOONS GROUND CINNAMON

1   TEASPOON GROUND CORIANDER

1   TEASPOON FRESHLY CRACKED BLACK
    PEPPER

½ TEASPOON TURMERIC

6   CUPS LOW-SODIUM BEEF BROTH

2   CUPS WATER

½ CUP CRACKED WHEAT BULGUR

1   15-OUNCE CAN CHICKPEAS, RINSED AND
    DRAINED

1   TABLESPOON FRESH LEMON JUICE

1   TEASPOON GRATED FRESH LEMON ZEST

¼ CUP SLICED FRESH MINT LEAVES

Cook the beef in a large saucepan set over medium-high heat, breaking up any chunks with the back of a spoon, for 5 minutes or until the beef is no longer pink. Add the onion. Season with salt and pepper. Cook and stir 5 minutes. Add the garlic, cumin, cinnamon, coriander, cracked pepper, and turmeric. Cook and stir 1 minute.

Add the broth, water, and bulgur to the pan. Bring to a boil. Reduce the heat to medium low and simmer 15 to 20 minutes, until the bulgur is tender.

Add the chickpeas, lemon juice, and lemon zest. Cook 3 to 4 minutes longer to blend flavors. Season with salt and pepper to taste. Serve topped with the mint. **Makes 6 servings.**

NUTRITION PER SERVING:
CALORIES 221; FAT 6.1G (SAT 2.9G, MONO 2.4G, POLY 0.7G);
PROTEIN 10.1G; CHOLESTEROL 5MG; SODIUM 219MG; CARBOHYDRATE 36.1G.

45 MINUTES

Asian Beef Noodle Soup

WITH CINNAMON & ANISE

No need to be anxious about this exotic-sounding soup. It's actually just an Asian twist on beef-noodle soup: tender beef, fragrant broth, and eminently slurpable noodles.

2 TEASPOONS TOASTED (DARK) SESAME OIL	2 CUPS WATER
6 GREEN ONIONS, TRIMMED AND CUT INTO 1½-INCH PIECES	2 TABLESPOONS TAMARI
6 CLOVES GARLIC, MINCED	2 TABLESPOONS UNSEASONED RICE VINEGAR
2 TABLESPOONS MINCED PEELED FRESH GINGER	8 OUNCES DRIED UDON NOODLES
2 TEASPOONS GROUND CINNAMON	1 MEDIUM BUNCH BOK CHOY, TRIMMED, WASHED, AND CUT INTO 1-INCH PIECES
1½ TEASPOONS ANISE SEEDS	½ POUND THINLY SLICED DELI ROAST BEEF, HALVED CROSSWISE AND CUT INTO STRIPS
1½ TEASPOONS ASIAN CHILE PASTE	½ CUP FRESH CILANTRO LEAVES
4 CUPS LOW-SODIUM BEEF BROTH	

Heat the oil in a heavy saucepan set over medium heat. Add the green onions, garlic, ginger, cinnamon, anise seeds, and chile paste. Cook and stir 1 minute.

Add the broth, water, tamari, and vinegar to the pan. Increase the heat to high and bring to a boil. Add the noodles and bok choy to the soup. Cook 7 to 10 minutes, until the noodles are cooked through and the bok choy is crisp-tender.

Stir in the roast beef and cook 1 minute to warm through. Season with salt and pepper to taste. Serve garnished with the cilantro. **Makes 6 servings.**

NUTRITION PER SERVING:
CALORIES 296; FAT 5.6G (SAT 1.8G, MONO 2.0G, POLY 0.4G);
PROTEIN 20.4G; CHOLESTEROL 39MG; SODIUM 407MG; CARBOHYDRATE 36.6G.

30 MINUTES

Beef & Snow Pea Soup

Toss away the takeout menu; you can make beef and snow peas in a ginger- and sesame-infused broth just as fast yourself.

1	CUP UNCOOKED WHITE RICE	10	OUNCES THINLY SLICED ROAST BEEF
4	CUPS LOW-SODIUM BEEF BROTH		(FROM THE DELI COUNTER), SLICED INTO
3	TABLESPOONS MINCED PEELED FRESH		½-INCH-WIDE STRIPS
	GINGER	4	GREEN ONIONS, TRIMMED AND THINLY
¾	POUND FRESH SNOW PEAS, CUT IN HALF		SLICED
	DIAGONALLY	2	TABLESPOONS LOW-SODIUM SOY SAUCE
1	LARGE RED BELL PEPPER, SEEDED AND	2	TABLESPOONS RICE VINEGAR
	CUT INTO VERY THIN STRIPS	1	TABLESPOON TOASTED (DARK) SESAME OIL

Cook the rice according to package directions.

While the rice cooks, place the broth and ginger in a large saucepan set over medium heat. Bring the broth to a simmer. Add the snow peas and red pepper and simmer 1 minute. Add the beef and green onions and cook 1 minute longer.

Remove the pan from the heat and stir in the soy sauce, vinegar, and sesame oil. Season the soup with salt and pepper to taste. Divide the cooked rice among 4 soup bowls and ladle the soup over the rice. **Makes 4 servings.**

NUTRITION PER SERVING:
CALORIES 173; FAT 5.1G (SAT 1.0G, MONO 1.5G, POLY 0.8G);
PROTEIN 10.1G; CHOLESTEROL 32MG; SODIUM 653MG; CARBOHYDRATE 22.8G.

20 MINUTES

Japanese Udon Beef Soup

This satisfying soup combines simplicity with deep, hearty flavors. Udon noodles are increasingly easy to find in well-stocked supermarkets, but whole grain linguine or fettuccine are fine substitutes.

8 OUNCES UNCOOKED UDON NOODLES (THICK, ROUND FRESH JAPANESE WHEAT NOODLES) OR WHOLE GRAIN LINGUINE OR FETTUCCINE

2 CLOVES GARLIC, MINCED

2 TABLESPOONS PEELED AND MINCED FRESH GINGER

¼ TEASPOON CAYENNE PEPPER

4 CUPS LOW-SODIUM BEEF BROTH

3 TABLESPOONS LOW-SODIUM SOY SAUCE

3 TABLESPOONS DRY SHERRY

1 TABLESPOON HONEY

1 TABLESPOON TOASTED (DARK) SESAME OIL

1 12-OUNCE PACKAGE SLICED MUSHROOMS

½ CUP THINLY SLICED CARROT

8 OUNCES TOP ROUND, TRIMMED AND THINLY SLICED

4 GREEN ONIONS, TRIMMED AND SLICED DIAGONALLY

1 5-OUNCE BAG PREWASHED BABY SPINACH

Cook the noodles according to the package directions; drain.

Meanwhile, place the garlic, ginger, cayenne, and broth in a large saucepan set over medium-high heat. Bring to a boil. Reduce heat to medium low and simmer 10 minutes.

Whisk the soy sauce, sherry, and honey in a small bowl.

Heat the sesame oil in a large nonstick skillet set over medium-high heat. Add the mushrooms and carrot. Cook and stir 2 minutes. Stir in the soy sauce mixture, then cook and stir 2 minutes.

Add the vegetable mixture to the broth mixture. Stir in the beef and cook 2 minutes or until the beef is no longer pink. Stir in the noodles, green onions, and spinach. Season with additional soy sauce to taste. Serve immediately. **Makes 5 servings.**

NUTRITION PER SERVING:
CALORIES 306; FAT 5.6G (SAT 1.8G, MONO 2.1G, POLY 0.4G);
PROTEIN 22.4G; CHOLESTEROL 48MG; SODIUM 507MG; CARBOHYDRATE 36.6G.

30 MINUTES

Enlightened Scotch Broth

Here I've taken a Scottish classic—hearty, meaty Scotch broth—and outfitted it for light, healthy, anytime eating. A key ingredient makes it work: ground lamb, which drastically cuts both the fat and overall cooking time compared to lamb stew meat.

1 POUND GROUND LAMB	2 TEASPOONS DRIED THYME
1 TABLESPOON CANOLA OIL	1 BAY LEAF
1½ CUPS CHOPPED ONION	4 CUPS LOW-SODIUM BEEF BROTH
2 LARGE CARROTS, PEELED AND DICED	1 CUP DARK BEER
4 CUPS SLICED KALE (OR MUSTARD GREEN LEAVES)	¾ CUP PEARL BARLEY
	1 TABLESPOON MALT OR CIDER VINEGAR

Cook the lamb in a large saucepan set over medium-high heat, breaking up any chunks with the back of a wooden spoon, 4 minutes or until the lamb is no longer pink. Transfer the lamb to a bowl with a slotted spoon. Wipe out the skillet with paper towels.

Heat the oil in the cleaned saucepan set over medium heat. Add the onion, carrots, kale, thyme, and bay leaf. Generously season with salt and pepper. Cook and stir 5 minutes.

Add the broth, beer, and barley. Simmer, covered, 35 minutes, until the barley is tender. Add the lamb and vinegar. Simmer, uncovered, 4 to 5 minutes to blend flavors. If needed, add water to the pan to thin the soup. Season with salt and pepper to taste. Remove and discard bay leaf. **Makes 6 servings.**

NUTRITION PER SERVING:
CALORIES 239; FAT 4.1G (SAT 1.2G, MONO 1.8G, POLY 0.8G);
PROTEIN 21.5G; CHOLESTEROL 45MG; SODIUM 530MG; CARBOHYDRATE 24.1G.

60 MINUTES

Lamb, Spinach & Couscous Soup

Forget the hours of simmering required when using whole pieces of stew meat or shoulder—the ground lamb in this soup not only turns meltingly tender following a brief browning and simmering, but is also a natural partner for the earthy-sweet flavor of the carrots, couscous, and spinach.

¾ POUND GROUND LAMB	2 TEASPOONS CRUMBLED DRIED ROSEMARY
1 TABLESPOON OLIVE OIL	2 4-OUNCE BAGS PREWASHED BABY
1½ CUPS CHOPPED ONION	SPINACH, COARSELY CHOPPED
3 LARGE GARLIC CLOVES, MINCED	½ CUP WHOLE WHEAT (OR REGULAR)
6 CUPS LOW-SODIUM BEEF BROTH	COUSCOUS
2 CUPS WATER	1 TABLESPOON FRESH LEMON JUICE
½ CUP DRY RED WINE	3 TABLESPOONS CHOPPED FRESH MINT
2 LARGE CARROTS, PEELED AND CHOPPED	LEAVES

Cook the ground lamb in a large, heavy saucepan set over medium-high heat, breaking up any chunks with the back of a spoon. Remove lamb with a slotted spoon to a paper-towel-lined plate. Wipe the pan clean.

Heat the oil in the cleaned pan set over medium-high heat. Add the onion. Season with salt and pepper. Cook and stir 5 minutes. Add the garlic. Cook and stir 1 minute.

Add the broth, water, wine, and carrots. Bring to a boil, skimming any froth off the surface. Reduce the heat to medium low and simmer 15 minutes, until the carrots are very tender.

Add the cooked lamb, rosemary, spinach, and couscous. Increase the heat to high and bring to a boil. Reduce the heat to medium low and cook 5 minutes or until the couscous is tender. Season with salt and pepper to taste. Mix in the lemon juice and mint. **Makes 6 servings.**

NUTRITION PER SERVING:
CALORIES 282; FAT 8.4G (SAT 2.9G, MONO 3.6G, POLY 0.6G);
PROTEIN 21.5G; CHOLESTEROL 54MG; SODIUM 353MG; CARBOHYDRATE 28.4G.

45 MINUTES

Portuguese Sausage, Sweet Potato & Spinach Soup

A more traditional version of this classic Portuguese soup would call for linguiça, a garlic-flavored Portuguese sausage, but to keep the soup streamlined, I use light smoked sausage in its place. But don't worry, it's still plenty rich and soothing. From the comfort of two kinds of potatoes to the bold flavors of smoked sausage and garlic, this soup has so much going on (with a short list of ingredients, to boot), it is a full meal in itself.

4 TEASPOONS OLIVE OIL, DIVIDED USE	2 POUNDS SWEET POTATOES, PEELED AND CUT INTO ¾-INCH CUBES
¾ OF A 16-OUNCE PACKAGE LIGHT SMOKED SAUSAGE, HALVED LENGTHWISE AND THINLY SLICED	1 POUND YUKON GOLD POTATOES, PEELED AND CUT INTO ¾-INCH CUBES
2 CUPS CHOPPED ONION	6 CUPS LOW-SODIUM CHICKEN BROTH
4 CLOVES GARLIC, MINCED	1 9- TO 10-OUNCE BAG FRESH SPINACH

Heat 2 teaspoons of the oil in a large saucepan set over medium-high heat. Add the sausage. Cook and stir 5 minutes, until the sausage is browned. Transfer the sausage to a paper-towel-lined plate.

Add the remaining 2 teaspoons of the oil to the pan. Add the onion. Season with salt and pepper, then cook and stir 5 minutes. Add the garlic. Cook and stir 1 minute.

Add the sweet potatoes, Yukon Gold potatoes, and broth. Bring to a boil, then reduce the heat to medium low, cover, and simmer until the potatoes are soft, stirring occasionally, about 25 minutes.

Using a potato masher, roughly mash half of the potatoes in the pan. Add the sausage and spinach. Simmer 4 to 5 minutes, until the spinach is wilted. Season with salt and pepper to taste. **Makes 8 servings.**

45 MINUTES

NUTRITION PER SERVING:
CALORIES 243; FAT 8.1G (SAT 2.7G, MONO 3.6G, POLY 0.9G); PROTEIN 26.4G; CHOLESTEROL 83MG; SODIUM 426MG; CARBOHYDRATE 13.6G.

Garlic Soup with Poached Eggs & Ham

The smoky heat of the pimentón contrasts pleasantly with the sweetness of the garlic in this soup. The ham, bread, and poached eggs make it substantial enough for a full meal.

1 TABLESPOON OLIVE OIL	½ TEASPOON HOT SMOKED PAPRIKA
1 LARGE HEAD OF GARLIC, CLOVES PEELED	(PIMENTÓN)
AND THINLY SLICED	4 LARGE EGGS, DIVIDED USE
2 CUPS DICED LEAN HAM	½ CUP PACKED SMALL FRESH CILANTRO
8 ½-INCH-THICK BAGUETTE SLICES	SPRIGS
4 CUPS LOW-SODIUM CHICKEN BROTH	4 LIME WEDGES

Heat the oil in a large saucepan set over medium heat. Add the garlic. Cook and stir 3 minutes. Add the ham and cook 3 to 5 minutes longer, until the garlic is golden brown. Transfer the garlic and ham to a bowl with a slotted spoon.

Add the bread slices to the saucepan and cook over medium heat, turning once, until browned, about 4 minutes. Divide the toasted bread among 4 large soup bowls.

Add the broth, smoked paprika, ham, and garlic to the pan and bring to a simmer. Break 1 egg into a cup and slide the egg into simmering stock. Repeat with remaining eggs. Poach eggs at a bare simmer until whites are firm but the yolks are softly set, about 4 to 5 minutes.

Transfer the eggs with slotted spoon to the toasted bread and season with salt. Ladle the soup into bowls and top with the cilantro. Serve with the lime wedges. **Makes 4 servings.**

Nutrition per Serving:
Calories 219; Fat 6.8g (sat 2.0g, mono 2.5g, poly 1.2g);
Protein 10.1g; Cholesterol 216mg; Sodium 270mg; Carbohydrate 28g.

30 MINUTES

Sausage and Kale Soup

This hearty soup gets its rich flavor from light smoked sausage and its substance from both red potatoes and meaty kale. In case you didn't know, the potatoes pack a punch of vitamin C and the kale a healthy dose of calcium.

4 TEASPOONS OLIVE OIL, DIVIDED USE	¼ TEASPOON CRUSHED RED PEPPER FLAKES
¾ OF A 16-OUNCE PACKAGE LIGHT SMOKED SAUSAGE, HALVED LENGTHWISE AND THINLY SLICED	1½ POUNDS RED POTATOES, PEELED AND CUT INTO ½-INCH CHUNKS
1½ CUPS CHOPPED ONION	5½ CUPS LOW-SODIUM CHICKEN BROTH
2 CLOVES GARLIC, MINCED	1 BUNCH KALE (ABOUT ¾ POUND), STEMMED AND SHREDDED

Heat 2 teaspoons of the oil in a large saucepan set over medium-high heat. Add the sausage. Cook and stir 5 minutes, until the sausage is browned. Transfer to a paper-towel-lined plate.

Heat the remaining 2 teaspoons of the oil in same pan set over medium-high heat. Add the onion. Season with salt and pepper. Cook and stir 5 minutes. Add the garlic and red pepper flakes. Cook and stir 1 minute.

Add the potatoes and broth to the pan. Bring to a boil, then reduce the heat and simmer 15 minutes or until the potatoes are tender.

Transfer half of the soup to a blender and purée until almost smooth. Return the soup to the pan and stir in the kale and sausage. Simmer 10 to 15 minutes, until the kale is wilted. Season with salt and pepper to taste. **Makes 4 servings.**

NUTRITION PER SERVING:
CALORIES 254; FAT 8.2G (SAT 2.1G, MONO 3.4G, POLY 1.4G);
PROTEIN 14.2G; CHOLESTEROL 27MG; SODIUM 567MG; CARBOHYDRATE 34.8G.

45 MINUTES

Shanghai Seared Pork & Noodle Soup

If you're craving an aromatic Chinatown-style noodle soup, this recipe is a quick fix. If you can't find rice noodles, substitute eight ounces of capellini, or angel hair pasta; cook it until al dente, according to package instructions.

½ POUND RICE STICK NOODLES	2 TABLESPOONS SHERRY
1 TABLESPOON CANOLA OIL	2 TEASPOONS RICE-WINE VINEGAR
¾ POUND PORK TENDERLOIN, TRIMMED OF FAT	2 MEDIUM CARROTS, PEELED AND CUT INTO MATCHSTICK STRIPS
1 12-OUNCE PACKAGE SLICED MUSHROOMS	½ HEAD NAPA CABBAGE, SHREDDED
2 GARLIC CLOVES, MINCED	2 GREEN ONIONS, TRIMMED AND THINLY SLICED
8 CUPS LOW-SODIUM BEEF BROTH	1 CUP BEAN SPROUTS
2 TABLESPOONS LOW-SODIUM SOY SAUCE	

Place the rice noodles in a large heatproof bowl; pour boiling water over the noodles. Let sit 8 to 10 minutes, until translucent but still slightly chewy. Drain.

Meanwhile, heat the oil in a large saucepan set over medium-high heat. Season the pork with salt and pepper. Sear the pork in pan until golden brown, 3 to 4 minutes. Sear other side, 3 to 4 minutes more. Remove the pork.

Reduce the heat to medium. Add the mushrooms and garlic to the pan. Season with salt and pepper. Cook and stir, scraping up any browned bits, 5 minutes.

Add the broth, soy sauce, sherry, and vinegar to the pan. Bring to a boil over medium-high heat. Cut the pork diagonally into very thin slices. Add to soup and cook 1 minute, until the pork is no longer pink. Remove from the heat and stir in the carrots, cabbage, green onions, and bean sprouts. Season with salt and pepper to taste.

Divide the noodles among 6 bowls and top with the soup. **Makes 6 servings.**

NUTRITION PER SERVING:
CALORIES 273; FAT 8.9G (SAT 1.9G, MONO 3.6G, POLY 2.0G);
PROTEIN 16.3G; CHOLESTEROL 38MG; SODIUM 399MG; CARBOHYDRATE 34.8G.

45 MINUTES

Rustic Sausage Soup

WITH PASTA & BEANS

Loaded with sausage, beans, and pasta, this easy soup can feed a small army—all in delicious style. It's a great addition to your weeknight repertoire.

¾ POUND ITALIAN SAUSAGES, CASINGS
    REMOVED

1½ CUPS CHOPPED ONION

4 MEDIUM CARROTS, PEELED AND CHOPPED

1 CUP CHOPPED CELERY

2 CLOVES GARLIC, MINCED

1½ TEASPOONS DRIED BASIL

1½ TEASPOONS DRIED ROSEMARY

½ TEASPOON DRIED RUBBED SAGE

¼ TEASPOON DRIED CRUSHED RED PEPPER

5 CUPS LOW-SODIUM CHICKEN BROTH

1 14.5-OUNCE CAN DICED TOMATOES,
    UNDRAINED

1 15-OUNCE CAN LIGHT RED KIDNEY BEANS,
    RINSED AND DRAINED

1 CUP UNCOOKED ELBOW MACARONI

OPTIONAL: ½ CUP CHOPPED FLAT-LEAF PARS-
    LEY LEAVES

Cook and stir the sausage in a large saucepan set over medium-high heat, breaking up chunks with back of a spoon, 5 minutes, until no longer pink. Add the onion, carrots, celery, garlic, basil, rosemary, sage, and red pepper. Season with salt and pepper. Cook and stir 8 minutes.

Add the broth, tomatoes with their juices, and beans. Bring the soup to a boil. Reduce the heat to medium low and simmer 20 minutes, until the vegetables are tender.

Add the macaroni to the soup and simmer until tender, about 15 minutes. Season with salt and pepper to taste. If desired, stir in the parsley. **Makes 8 servings.**

NUTRITION PER SERVING:
CALORIES 254; FAT 9.2G (SAT 2.9G, MONO 3.2G, POLY 2.7G);
PROTEIN 21.0G; CHOLESTEROL 74MG; SODIUM 929MG; CARBOHYDRATE 21.2G.

60 MINUTES

Puerto Rican Ham Soup

WITH PIGEON PEAS & SOFRITO

Peas (or beans) are staples at the Puerto Rican table, and this soup is at once pull-out-the-stops special and everyday. You won't believe how much flavor can be packed into such an understated soup. The secret is an abundantly seasoned sofrito—the flavor base of onion, spices, and tomato—as well as tender sweet potatoes and a handful of lean diced ham.

2 14-OUNCE PACKAGES FROZEN (THAWED) PIGEON PEAS OR BLACK-EYED PEAS	½ CUP FINELY CHOPPED FRESH CILANTRO LEAVES
6 CUPS LOW-SODIUM CHICKEN BROTH	1 SMALL ROMA TOMATO, SEEDED AND CHOPPED
2 TEASPOONS CANOLA OIL	1 TEASPOON DRIED THYME LEAVES
1 CUP FINELY CHOPPED ONION	1½ CUPS DICED LEAN HAM
1 MEDIUM RED BELL PEPPER, SEEDED AND FINELY CHOPPED	1 MEDIUM SWEET POTATO, PEELED AND FINELY DICED
1 LARGE FRESH JALAPEÑO CHILE, SEEDED AND FINELY CHOPPED	1 TEASPOON RED WINE VINEGAR
4 CLOVES GARLIC, MINCED	

Place the peas and broth in a large saucepan set over medium-high heat. Bring to a boil, then reduce heat to medium low and simmer 25 minutes, uncovered.

While the peas simmer, make the sofrito: Heat the oil in a large skillet set over medium-high heat. Add the onion, bell pepper, jalapeño, and garlic. Cook and stir 5 minutes. Add the cilantro, tomato, and thyme. Season with salt and pepper. Cook and stir 4 minutes.

Stir the sofrito, ham, and sweet potato into the pea mixture and simmer 20 minutes, uncovered, until the sweet potato is tender. Stir in the vinegar and season with salt and pepper to taste. **Makes 8 servings.**

NUTRITION PER SERVING:
CALORIES 251; FAT 4.9G (SAT 1.5G, MONO 1.7G, POLY 0.8G);
PROTEIN 13.4G; CHOLESTEROL 46MG; SODIUM 512MG; CARBOHYDRATE 37.7G.

60 MINUTES

Swedish Yellow Split-Pea Soup

WITH HAM & FRESH DILL

Yellow pea soup with ham is traditionally served every Thursday night in Sweden. (If you've ever wondered why bags of yellow split peas are sold at IKEA, now you know.) After eating the soup everyone fills up on Swedish pancakes. I recommend trying the pancakes, too (with plenty of berry preserves on top).

1   TABLESPOON OLIVE OIL

2   LARGE LEEKS (WHITE AND PALE GREEN
    PARTS ONLY), CHOPPED

2   MEDIUM CARROTS, PEELED AND CHOPPED

1⅓ CUPS YELLOW SPLIT PEAS, RINSED

6   CUPS LOW-SODIUM CHICKEN BROTH

¾   CUP WATER

1½ CUPS FINELY DICED LEAN HAM

3   TABLESPOONS CHOPPED FRESH DILL,
    DIVIDED USE

Heat the oil in heavy, large pot over medium-high heat. Add the leeks and carrots. Season with salt and pepper. Cook and stir 5 minutes.

Stir in the split peas and broth. Bring to a boil. Reduce heat to medium low. Cover and simmer until peas are just tender, about 35 minutes. Remove from the heat.

Transfer 1 cup soup solids and the broth to a blender. Purée until smooth. Return purée to the soup. Stir in the ham and 2 tablespoons of the dill. Cook 5 minutes longer to blend flavors. Thin the soup with water if it's too thick. Season with salt and pepper to taste. Serve sprinkled with the remaining dill. **Makes 6 servings.**

NUTRITION PER SERVING:
CALORIES 233; FAT 3.5G (SAT 1.1G, MONO 1.6G, POLY 0.5G);
PROTEIN 13.7G; CHOLESTEROL 4.1MG; SODIUM 359MG; CARBOHYDRATE 38.7G.

60
MINUTES

Cassoulet Soup

One taste of this deeply flavored, soul-satisfying soup and you'll understand why it's a French classic. Most versions of cassoulet are closer to a stew, but my soup variation is every bit as delicious and fulfilling. If you like, top each serving of soup with toasted breadcrumbs or a piece of toasted rustic bread, both of which are traditional options.

1 TABLESPOON OLIVE OIL	2 15-OUNCE CAN CANNELLINI (WHITE KID-NEY BEANS) OR GREAT NORTHERN BEANS, DRAINED, DIVIDED USE
1½ CUPS CHOPPED ONION	
¾ OF A 16-OUNCE PACKAGE LIGHT SMOKED SAUSAGE, DICED	
2 TEASPOONS DRIED THYME	2 CUPS DICED CHICKEN (E.G., FROM A PUR-CHASED ROTISSERIE CHICKEN)
1 CUP DRY WHITE WINE	¼ CUP CHOPPED FRESH FLAT-LEAF PARSLEY LEAVES
4 CUPS LOW-SODIUM CHICKEN BROTH	
1 14.5-OUNCE CAN DICED TOMATOES, UNDRAINED	

Heat the oil in a large saucepan set over medium-high heat. Add the onion and sausage. Cook and stir 5 minutes. Add the thyme and stir 1 minute.

Add the wine to the pan. Bring to a boil. Continue to boil 2 minutes, until the liquid is slightly reduced. Reduce the heat to medium low and add the broth, tomatoes with their juices, 1 can of the beans, and the chicken. Cook 5 minutes.

In a small bowl mash the remaining can of beans to a coarse purée using a fork. Add to the soup. Partially cover the pan and simmer 10 minutes to meld flavors. Season with salt and pepper to taste. Sprinkle with the parsley and serve. **Makes 6 servings.**

NUTRITION PER SERVING:
CALORIES 231; FAT 6.1G (SAT 2.2G, MONO 1.9G, POLY 1.3G);
PROTEIN 22.1G; CHOLESTEROL 50MG; SODIUM 517MG; CARBOHYDRATE 25.8G.

30 MINUTES

6. LEGUME & GRAIN

Soups

HEARTY BROWN RICE, SPINACH & MUSHROOM SOUP, PASTA E FAGIOLI SOUP, BLACK BEAN SOUP WITH PUMPKIN, LIME & CHIPOTLE, AVGOLÉMONO (GREEK LEMON & RICE SOUP), MUSHROOM, BARLEY & BACON SOUP, KAMUT & CHICKPEA SOUP WITH FRESH HERBS, RED BEANS & RICE SOUP, CURRIED BLACK-EYED PEA SOUP, TUNISIAN CHICKPEA SOUP, BEAN & BACON SOUP, TUSCAN FARRO & BEAN SOUP, WEST AFRICAN PEANUT SOUP, FRENCH LENTIL SOUP, SOUTHERN BARLEY, HAM & GREENS SOUP, WILD RICE & CORN SOUP WITH CAJUN SPICES, THAI COCONUT & JASMINE RICE SOUP, EDAMAME SUCCOTASH SOUP, RED LENTIL MULLIGATAWNY, SOUTHWESTERN BLACK BEAN & RICE SOUP, WHITE BEAN & BASIL SOUP, SPLIT-PEA SOUP WITH CARAMELIZED ONIONS, QUINOA & GARDEN VEGETABLE SOUP, AND RISOTTO PRIMAVERA SOUP

Hearty Brown Rice, Spinach & Mushroom Soup

Some soups genuinely do inspire fidelity akin to love, and this is one of them. In the cold of winter, when I mull over the matter of what soup to cook up in my Saturday morning kitchen to provide comfort all weekend long, I decide with remarkable frequency to make this one.

1¼ CUPS UNCOOKED BROWN RICE

1 TABLESPOON OLIVE OIL

1½ CUPS CHOPPED ONION

2 CLOVES GARLIC, MINCED

1 12-OUNCE PACKAGE SLICED MUSHROOMS

6 CUPS LOW-SODIUM CHICKEN OR VEGETABLE BROTH

1 TEASPOON DRIED ROSEMARY, CRUMBLED

1 15-OUNCE CAN CHICKPEAS (GARBANZO BEANS), RINSED AND DRAINED

1 10-OUNCE BAG PREWASHED SPINACH LEAVES, COARSELY CHOPPED

½ CUP FRESHLY GRATED PARMESAN CHEESE

In a large saucepan, bring 3 cups water to a boil. Stir in the brown rice and return to a boil; reduce to a simmer. Cook, covered, for 30 minutes.

Meanwhile, heat the oil in a large saucepan set over medium-high heat. Add the onion. Season with salt and pepper. Cook and stir 5 minutes. Add the garlic and mushrooms. Cook and stir 5 minutes longer. Add the broth and rosemary. Bring to a boil. Cover and remove from the heat.

Check the rice after 30 minutes; if it is not yet tender, cover and continue cooking, up to 10 more minutes. Stir the rice (and any remaining liquid) and the chickpeas into the broth. Return to a boil over medium-high heat. Reduce the heat to low. Cover and simmer 5 minutes to blend flavors.

Stir in the spinach. Cook, uncovered, 1 to 2 minutes, until the spinach is just wilted. Season with salt and pepper to taste. Serve the soup sprinkled with the Parmesan cheese. **Makes 6 servings.**

60 MINUTES

NUTRITION PER SERVING:
CALORIES 217; FAT 4.7G (SAT 1.0G, MONO 2.1G, POLY 1.1G);
PROTEIN 13.9G; CHOLESTEROL 20MG; SODIUM 438MG; CARBOHYDRATE 31.1G.

Pasta e Fagioli

Pasta e fagioli, also known as pasta fazool (and many other variations on the spelling), is pure comfort soup that almost everyone loves; thus, a tremendous number of local variations on the theme exist, both in Italy and here in the United States. Mine has all of the favorite flavors with a fraction of the fat and calories.

1 CUP CHOPPED ONION	6 CUPS LOW-SODIUM CHICKEN OR VEGETABLE BROTH
2 BACON SLICES, CHOPPED	
2 TEASPOONS MINCED GARLIC	2 15-OUNCE CANS LIGHT RED KIDNEY BEANS, RINSED AND DRAINED
1 TABLESPOON CHOPPED FRESH OR 1½ TEASPOONS DRIED ROSEMARY	¾ CUP SMALL ELBOW MACARONI
1¼ TEASPOONS DRIED THYME LEAVES	1 CUP JARRED GOOD-QUALITY MARINARA SAUCE
1 BAY LEAF	
¼ TEASPOON RED PEPPER FLAKES	⅓ CUP FRESHLY GRATED PARMESAN CHEESE

Place the onion and bacon in a heavy, large saucepan set over medium-high heat. Season with salt and pepper. Cook and stir 5 minutes. Add the garlic, rosemary, thyme, bay leaf, and red pepper flakes. Cook and stir 2 minutes.

Add the broth and beans. Cover and bring to a boil. Reduce the heat to medium and simmer 10 minutes. Transfer 1½ cups of the bean mixture to a blender. Purée until smooth.

Add the macaroni to the pan and boil 8 minutes, covered, until tender but still firm to the bite.

Add the purée and the marinara sauce to the pan, stirring. Cook 2 minutes to warm through. Season with salt and pepper to taste. Serve the soup sprinkled with the Parmesan cheese. **Makes 6 servings.**

NUTRITION PER SERVING:
CALORIES 315; FAT 6.9G (SAT 2.0G, MONO 3.9G, POLY 0.9G);
PROTEIN 16.1G; CHOLESTEROL 4MG; SODIUM 513MG; CARBOHYDRATE 46G.

45 MINUTES

Black Bean Soup

WITH PUMPKIN, LIME & CHIPOTLE

Your search for the best black bean soup has ended. Sorry, I just can't be humble about this soup, it's that good. You don't taste the pumpkin—it just makes it extra thick and voluptuous (as well as extra nutritious). Chipotle and cumin add smoky undertones that are brightened with the additions of lime and cilantro. It freezes beautifully, enough for a great dinner and several soul-soothing lunches to follow. You don't need much more to round out the meal except, perhaps, some cornbread. It will warm you through and through!

3	15-OUNCE CANS BLACK BEANS, RINSED AND DRAINED	2	TEASPOONS DRIED OREGANO
1	15-OUNCE CAN DICED TOMATOES, UNDRAINED	1	TEASPOON SALT
2	TABLESPOONS OLIVE OIL	4¼	CUPS LOW-SODIUM CHICKEN OR VEGETABLE BROTH
1¾	CUPS FINELY CHOPPED ONION	1	15-OUNCE CAN SOLID PACK PUMPKIN
4	CLOVES GARLIC, MINCED	3	TABLESPOONS FRESH LIME JUICE
1½	TABLESPOONS GROUND CUMIN	¾	CUP PLAIN NONFAT YOGURT
1	TABLESPOON CHOPPED CANNED CHIPOTLE CHILES		OPTIONAL: ¼ CUP CHOPPED FRESH CILANTRO LEAVES (OR CHIVES)

In a food processor coarsely purée the beans and tomatoes with their juices.

Heat the oil in a large saucepan set over medium-high heat. Add the onion. Cook and stir 5 minutes. Add the garlic, cumin, chipotle chiles, oregano, and salt. Cook and stir 1 minute.

Stir in the bean purée, broth, and pumpkin until blended. Reduce the heat to medium low and simmer, uncovered, stirring occasionally, 25 minutes.

Just before serving, stir in the lime juice. Season with salt and pepper to taste. Serve garnished with dollops of the yogurt and cilantro. **Makes 8 servings.**

Camilla's Note: Chipotle chiles come in a small can, packed in a spicy tomato sauce (adobo). You can save the remaining chiles by spacing out each of the remaining chiles, with a spoonful of sauce, on a parchment-lined baking sheet. Freeze until firm, then pop them off the sheet and store in a ziplock bag in the freezer.

NUTRITION PER SERVING:
CALORIES 170; FAT 3.6G (SAT 0.6G; POLY 0.4G, MONO 2.5G);
PROTEIN 9.8G; CHOLESTEROL 0.5MG; SODIUM 910.1MG; CARBOHYDRATE 30.1G.

45 MINUTES

Avgolémono

(GREEK LEMON & RICE SOUP)

Avgolémono is Greek for egg-lemon and can refer to a range of sauces as well as the soup. It is made with egg yolks and lemon juice mixed with broth, heated until the yolks thicken but before they boil, so the egg doesn't curdle. Variations are extensive and the soup can be as thick as a stew or very brothy, but mine is a version that is very common: still light, but made more substantial with the addition of rice.

---

6   CUPS LOW-SODIUM CHICKEN OR
    VEGETABLE BROTH

½   CUP UNCOOKED LONG GRAIN WHITE RICE

4   LARGE EGGS

¼   CUP FRESH LEMON JUICE

¼   CUP SNIPPED FRESH CHIVES OR GREEN
    ONIONS

Place the broth in a large saucepan set over high heat. Bring to a boil. Add the rice. Reduce heat to medium low. Cover and cook 20 minutes. Remove the pan from heat.

In a medium bowl beat the eggs and lemon juice with a fork or electric mixer set on low until foamy. Beat half of the hot soup into the eggs, ½ cup at a time. Stir the egg mixture into the remaining soup.

Cook over very low heat 3 minutes. Season with salt and pepper to taste. Serve with chives sprinkled atop soup. **Makes 4 servings.**

NUTRITION PER SERVING:
CALORIES 117; FAT 2.9G (SAT 1.1G, MONO 0.5G, POLY 0.3G);
PROTEIN 8.1G; CHOLESTEROL 106MG; SODIUM 365MG; CARBOHYDRATE 10G.

30 MINUTES

Mushroom, Barley & Bacon Soup

Barley is one of the oldest grains on the planet. It has a mild sweetness and, when cooked properly, a chewy but tender texture. Pearled barley is the most widely available and the easiest to cook. It has been abraded many times to remove the tough outer husk, and this lightens it to a buff color. It cooks up quickly here, absorbing the earthy flavor of the mushrooms—delectable. A splash of red wine vinegar at the end of the cooking enlivens the flavors.

3 SLICES BACON, CHOPPED	4 CUPS LOW-SODIUM BEEF OR VEGETABLE BROTH
1¾ CUPS CHOPPED ONION	
3 CLOVES GARLIC, MINCED	1 CUP PEARL BARLEY
1 POUND BUTTON OR CRIMINI MUSHROOMS, TRIMMED AND HALVED	1 TEASPOON DRIED OREGANO
	3 CUPS WATER
2 TABLESPOONS TOMATO PASTE	1 TEASPOON RED WINE VINEGAR
	¼ CUP CHOPPED FRESH PARSLEY LEAVES

Cook the bacon in a large pot set over medium-high heat 3 to 5 minutes, until crisp. Reduce the heat to medium.

Add the onion and garlic. Season with salt and pepper. Cook and stir 5 minutes. Add the mushrooms. Cook and stir 6 minutes. Stir in the tomato paste and cook 1 minute more.

Add the broth, barley, oregano, and water. Bring to a boil. Reduce the heat to medium low and simmer, partially covered, 35 to 40 minutes, until the barley is tender. Add more water to thin the soup, as needed.

Stir in the vinegar. Season with salt and pepper to taste. Serve sprinkled with the parsley. **Makes 6 servings.**

Vegetarian Option: Heat 1½ tablespoons olive oil in the pan in place of the bacon and proceed as directed.

NUTRITION PER SERVING:
CALORIES 175; FAT 5.2G (SAT 2.4G, MONO 1.5G, POLY 0.8G);
PROTEIN 8.1G; CHOLESTEROL 38MG; SODIUM 501MG; CARBOHYDRATE 26G.

60 MINUTES

Kamut & Chickpea Soup

WITH FRESH HERBS

Kamut is both a delicious and remarkable grain. It's an ancient relative of modern durum wheat, but about two to three times larger with 20 to 40 percent more protein, as well as significantly more healthy fats, amino acids, vitamins, and minerals. As for taste, it is slightly sweet, with a rich, buttery flavor. It used to be very hard to find, but now it's available in the health food section of well-stocked grocery stores. But if you cannot find it, you can substitute an equal amount of spelt, grano, wheat berries, or pearl barley. And although this soup is delectable on day one, it gets even better as it sits.

¾ CUP KAMUT BERRIES, RINSED

2 CUPS BOILING WATER

2 TABLESPOONS OLIVE OIL

2 CUPS FINELY CHOPPED ONION

1 CUP FINELY CHOPPED CARROT

1 SMALL FENNEL BULB, TRIMMED AND CHOPPED (RESERVE FENNEL FRONDS)

3 CLOVES GARLIC, MINCED

2 TABLESPOONS CHOPPED FRESH TARRAGON LEAVES

8 CUPS LOW-SODIUM CHICKEN OR VEGETABLE BROTH

2 BAY LEAVES

⅓ CUP DRIED LENTILS

¾ CUP CHOPPED FRESH PARSLEY LEAVES

1 15-OUNCE CAN CHICKPEAS (GARBANZO BEANS), RINSED AND DRAINED

Place the kamut in a small bowl. Slowly pour the boiling water over the kamut. Let stand 25 minutes. Drain any excess water.

Meanwhile, heat the oil in a large saucepan set over medium heat. Add the onion, carrot, and fennel. Season with salt and pepper. Cook and stir 10 minutes. Add the garlic and tarragon. Cook and stir 1 minute.

Add the kamut, broth, bay leaves, lentils, and parsley. Increase heat to high. Bring to a boil. Reduce the heat to medium low, cover, and simmer 30 minutes. Discard the bay leaves. Add the chickpeas. Simmer 2 minutes. Season with salt and pepper to taste. Serve topped with minced fennel fronds, if desired. **Makes 6 servings.**

NUTRITION PER SERVING:

CALORIES 298; FAT 7.1G (SAT 1.1G, MONO 4.3G, POLY 1.2G);

PROTEIN 15.2G; CHOLESTEROL 0MG; SODIUM 521MG; CARBOHYDRATE 32.4G.

60 MINUTES

Red Beans & Rice Soup

Cooking red beans and rice on wash-day Mondays is an old Louisiana custom. Families would simmer a pot of beans all day while they did laundry. My variation comes together quickly, but you may still be able to get a load through the wash cycle by the time soup's on.

1 TABLESPOON CANOLA OIL	½ TEASPOON GROUND CUMIN
1½ CUPS CHOPPED ONION	½ TEASPOON HOT SAUCE
¾ CUP CHOPPED CELERY	1 14.5-OUNCE CAN CHILI-READY DICED
2 CLOVES GARLIC, MINCED	TOMATOES, UNDRAINED
2 TABLESPOONS ALL-PURPOSE FLOUR	1 15-OUNCE CAN LIGHT RED KIDNEY BEANS,
4 CUPS LOW-SODIUM VEGETABLE BROTH	RINSED AND DRAINED
⅔ CUP UNCOOKED LONG GRAIN WHITE RICE	1 6-OUNCE CAN TINY SHRIMP, DRAINED
1 TABLESPOON CHILI POWDER	1 TEASPOON BALSAMIC OR RED WINE
1 TEASPOON DRIED THYME LEAVES	VINEGAR

Heat the oil in a large saucepan set over medium heat. Add the onion and celery. Season with salt and pepper. Cook and stir 5 minutes. Add the garlic. Cook and stir 1 minute. Sprinkle the vegetables with the flour. Cook and stir 1 minute more.

Add the broth, rice, chili powder, thyme, cumin, hot sauce, and tomatoes with their juices. Bring to a boil. Reduce the heat to medium low, cover, and cook 20 minutes.

Add the beans and shrimp to the rice mixture, and stir well. Simmer 2 minutes. Remove the pan from the heat and stir in the vinegar. Season with salt and pepper to taste. **Makes 6 servings.**

NUTRITION PER SERVING:
CALORIES 224; FAT 4.4G (SAT 1.8G, MONO 1.1G, POLY 0.9G);
PROTEIN 11.4G; CHOLESTEROL 8MG; SODIUM 326MG; CARBOHYDRATE 36.3G.

45 MINUTES

Curried Black-Eyed Pea Soup

I like beans a lot, but I love black-eyed peas. Also known as cow peas, they are thought to have originated in North Africa, where they have been eaten for centuries. Here they pack a spicy broth with plenty of folate, while onions infuse the soup with vitamin C. And that cilantro is more than green garnish: one small serving delivers an amazingly high amount of vitamin A and lutein.

2 BACON SLICES, CHOPPED	2 15-OUNCE CANS BLACK-EYED PEAS, RINSED AND DRAINED
1¼ CUPS CHOPPED ONION	
¾ CUP CHOPPED CELERY	6 CUPS LOW-SODIUM CHICKEN OR VEGETABLE BROTH
2 TEASPOONS MILD CURRY POWDER	
½ TEASPOON GROUND CUMIN	¼ CUP CHOPPED FRESH CILANTRO LEAVES
¼ TEASPOON CAYENNE PEPPER	

Cook the bacon in a large saucepan set over medium-high heat 5 to 6 minutes, until crisp.

Add the onion, celery, curry, cumin, and cayenne. Cook and stir 8 minutes. Add the peas and broth and simmer 10 minutes.

Transfer 2 cups of the soup solids to a blender and purée until smooth. Return the purée to the pan. Season the soup with salt and pepper. Cook 3 to 4 minutes longer to blend flavors. Season with salt and pepper to taste. Serve sprinkled with the cilantro. **Makes 6 servings.**

NUTRITION PER SERVING:
CALORIES 141; FAT 3.6G (SAT 2.1G, MONO 0.9G, POLY 0.4G);
PROTEIN 11.9G; CHOLESTEROL 15MG; SODIUM 603MG; CARBOHYDRATE 17.6G.

30 MINUTES

Tunisian Chickpea Soup

This recipe proves you don't need meat to make a hearty soup. Several spices give this chickpea and lentil soup rich flavor without lamb, the traditional meat used in many Tunisian soups and stews. For a simple and delicious complement, pair the soup with baked pita wedges.

1 TABLESPOON OLIVE OIL	2 15-OUNCE CANS CHICKPEAS (GARBANZO BEANS), UNDRAINED
1½ CUPS FINELY CHOPPED ONION	7 CUPS LOW-SODIUM CHICKEN OR VEGETABLE BROTH
1½ CUPS FINELY CHOPPED FENNEL (ABOUT 1 MEDIUM BULB)	1 CUP LENTILS
2 TEASPOONS TURMERIC	½ CUP ORZO (RICE-SHAPED PASTA) OR OTHER SMALL-SHAPED PASTA
1½ TEASPOONS GROUND CUMIN	⅔ CUP CHOPPED FRESH CILANTRO LEAVES, DIVIDED USE
1½ TEASPOONS GROUND CINNAMON	½ CUP CHOPPED FRESH PARSLEY LEAVES
1¼ TEASPOONS HOT SMOKED PAPRIKA (PIMENTÓN)	2 TABLESPOONS FRESH LEMON JUICE
1 28-OUNCE CAN CRUSHED TOMATOES, UNDRAINED	

Heat the oil in a large saucepan set over medium-high heat. Add the onion and fennel. Season with salt and pepper. Cook and stir 8 minutes. Add the turmeric, cumin, cinnamon, and smoked paprika. Cook and stir 2 minutes.

Stir in the crushed tomatoes with their juices, chickpeas, vegetable broth, and lentils. Bring to a boil, then reduce heat and simmer, uncovered, until the lentils are tender, about 30 minutes.

Stir in the pasta and ⅓ cup of the cilantro. Cook, stirring occasionally, 10 minutes, until the pasta is tender. Stir in the parsley, lemon juice, and the remaining ⅓ cup cilantro. Season with salt and pepper to taste. **Makes 8 servings.**

NUTRITION PER SERVING:
CALORIES 214; FAT 6.7G (SAT 1.1G, MONO 3.7G, POLY 1.1G);
PROTEIN 12.2G; CHOLESTEROL 60MG; SODIUM 516MG; CARBOHYDRATE 23.1G.

60 MINUTES

Bean & Bacon Soup

This is one of my favorite soups of childhood. My Dad would gather my siblings and me around the kitchen table on Saturday afternoons and we would eat it with as many saltines crackers as we wanted. It sounds simple, but I thought it was grand. I've put my hand to making a home-made version, and am pleased as punch with the results. The molasses and mustard may sound odd, but trust me: They add a color and subtle notes of sweetness and piquancy that make the soup special.

3 BACON SLICES, CHOPPED	2 15-OUNCE CANS GREAT NORTHERN BEANS, DRAINED
1¼ CUPS CHOPPED ONION	2 CUPS WATER
1 CUP PEELED AND FINELY CHOPPED CARROT	1 TABLESPOON DARK MOLASSES
1 CUP FINELY CHOPPED CELERY	2 TEASPOONS DIJON MUSTARD
4 CLOVES GARLIC, MINCED	

Cook the bacon in a large saucepan set over medium-high heat 5 to 6 minutes, until crisp. Use a slotted spoon to transfer the bacon to a paper-towel-lined plate. Discard all but 1 tablespoon fat from the pan.

Reduce the heat to medium. Add the onion, carrot, and celery. Cook and stir 10 minutes. Add the garlic and cook 2 minutes more. Add the beans, water, molasses, and mustard. Increase the heat to high and bring to a boil. Reduce the heat to low and simmer, covered, 10 minutes.

Uncover and, with a potato masher or large slotted spoon, partially mash the bean mixture until the soup thickens slightly. Season with salt and pepper to taste. **Makes 6 servings.**

NUTRITION PER SERVING:
CALORIES 162; FAT 4.8G (SAT 2.2G, MONO 1.8G, POLY 0.5G);
PROTEIN 8.3G; CHOLESTEROL 10MG; SODIUM 440MG; CARBOHYDRATE 20.6G.

45 MINUTES

Tuscan Farro & Bean Soup

Farro is an ancient variety of wheat cultivated in Italy that has recently caught the attention of cooks in the United States. It has a nutty flavor and a firm, chewy texture that resembles barley more than wheat. Italians put farro in salads, stuffings, and especially in soups. Be sure to buy whole-grain farro as opposed to the cracked form; the latter looks more like bulgur, has a very different texture, and cooks much faster.

2 TABLESPOONS OLIVE OIL	½ CUP LOOSELY PACKED FRESH FLAT-LEAF
1½ CUPS CHOPPED ONION	PARSLEY LEAVES, DIVIDED USE
1 CUP PEELED, CHOPPED CARROT	1 15-OUNCE CAN GREAT NORTHERN OR
2 CLOVES GARLIC, MINCED	OTHER WHITE BEANS, UNDRAINED
1 TABLESPOON DRY RUBBED SAGE	1 CUP WHOLE-GRAIN FARRO
1½ TEASPOONS DRIED THYME LEAVES	2 TEASPOONS RED WINE VINEGAR
1 14.5-OUNCE CAN DICED TOMATOES,	½ TEASPOON FRESHLY CRACKED BLACK
UNDRAINED	PEPPER
7 CUPS LOW-SODIUM CHICKEN OR	
VEGETABLE BROTH, DIVIDED USE	

Heat the oil in a large saucepan set over medium-high heat. Add the onion and carrot. Season with salt and pepper. Cook and stir 5 minutes. Stir in the garlic, sage, thyme, tomatoes with their juices, 2 cups of the broth, and ¼ cup of the parsley. Bring to a boil, then reduce heat and simmer, partially covered, 10 minutes.

Blend the mixture in batches in a blender until smooth. Return to the pan. Purée the beans with 1 of the remaining cups of the broth. Add to pan along with the remaining 4 cups of the broth.

Bring the soup to a boil. Add the farro, then reduce the heat to medium low. Cook, stirring occasionally, 30 minutes, until the farro is tender (it should be slightly chewy). Stir in the vinegar and pepper. Season with salt to taste. Serve sprinkled with the remaining parsley. **Makes 8 servings.**

Camilla's Note: If you cannot find farro, pearl barley is an excellent substitute.

60

MINUTES

NUTRITION PER SERVING:
CALORIES 232; FAT 7.9G (SAT 1.2G, MONO 4.9G, POLY 1.1G);
PROTEIN 7.9G; CHOLESTEROL 0MG; SODIUM 537MG; CARBOHYDRATE 35.3G.

West African Peanut Soup

Various peanut soups are common throughout Africa. Some are very simple, others more elaborate. Many contain chicken, goat, or fish, but I've kept my interpretation vegetarian, but still hearty, thanks to the addition of sweet potatoes. For a richer variation, consider substituting 1 cup canned light coconut milk—brought to a boil—in place of the boiling water. Delicious!

1 TABLESPOON CANOLA OIL	1 14.5-OUNCE CAN DICED TOMATOES, UNDRAINED
1¼ CUPS CHOPPED ONION	
1½ CUPS PEELED AND DICED SWEET POTATO (ABOUT HALF OF 1 MEDIUM SWEET POTATO)	3 CUPS LOW-SODIUM CHICKEN OR VEGETABLE BROTH
½ CUP SEEDED AND CHOPPED GREEN PEPPER	1 CUP BOILING WATER
2 CLOVES GARLIC, MINCED	⅓ CUP CREAMY PEANUT BUTTER (DO NOT USE OLD-FASHIONED OR NATURAL VARIETIES)
2 TEASPOONS MILD CURRY POWDER	
¾ TEASPOON GROUND CUMIN	6 TABLESPOONS CHOPPED FRESH CILANTRO LEAVES, DIVIDED USE

Heat the oil in a large saucepan set over medium-high heat. Add the onion, sweet potato, and green pepper. Season with salt and pepper. Cook and stir 5 minutes. Add the garlic, curry powder, and cumin. Cook and stir 1 minute.

Add the tomatoes with their juices and broth. Bring to a boil, then reduce the heat to medium low. Cook, partially covered, 15 minutes, until sweet potatoes are tender.

With a potato masher or large slotted spoon, partially mash the sweet potatoes. Stir the boiling water into the peanut butter until smooth, then add to the soup. Stir in half of the cilantro. Simmer, uncovered, 5 minutes. Season with salt and pepper to taste. Serve sprinkled with the remaining cilantro. **Makes 4 servings.**

NUTRITION PER SERVING:
CALORIES 158; FAT 5.1G (SAT 1.2G, MONO 2.1G, POLY 1.3G);
PROTEIN 6.2G; CHOLESTEROL 21MG; SODIUM 397MG; CARBOHYDRATE 19.3G.

45 MINUTES

French Lentil Soup

It won't take more than a spoonful or two to convince you why this soup is a French classic. Soaking the lentils in hot water helps them cook a bit more quickly when they're added to the soup. Leftovers are great, as most legume soups benefit from being made a day ahead so their flavors meld. Stir in a little water when you reheat the soup if it's too thick.

2 CUPS BOILING WATER	2 TEASPOONS CHOPPED FRESH OR
1¼ CUPS FRENCH (GREEN) OR	1 TEASPOON DRIED ROSEMARY
REGULAR LENTILS	1 14.5-OUNCE CAN CRUSHED TOMATOES,
1½ TABLESPOONS OLIVE OIL	UNDRAINED
2 CUPS CHOPPED ONION	5 CUPS LOW-SODIUM CHICKEN OR
1 CUP CHOPPED CELERY	VEGETABLE BROTH
1 CUP CHOPPED CARROTS	2 TEASPOONS BALSAMIC VINEGAR
3 CLOVES GARLIC, MINCED	GARNISH: CHOPPED CELERY LEAVES

Pour the boiling water over the lentils in a medium bowl. Let stand 10 minutes.

Meanwhile, heat the oil in a large saucepan set over medium-high heat. Add the onion, celery, and carrots. Season with salt and pepper. Cook and stir 10 minutes, until the vegetables begin to brown. Add the garlic and rosemary. Cook 1 minute longer.

Drain the lentils and add them to pan along with the tomatoes with their juices and broth. Bring to boil. Reduce the heat to medium low. Cover and simmer 35 minutes, until the lentils are tender.

Transfer 2 cups of the soup (mostly solids) to blender and purée until smooth. Return the purée to the soup in the pan. Stir in the vinegar and season with salt and pepper to taste. Simmer 5 minutes longer. Serve garnished with the chopped celery leaves. **Makes 6 servings.**

NUTRITION PER SERVING:
CALORIES 214; FAT 4.6G (SAT 1.1G, MONO 2.8G, POLY 0.7G);
PROTEIN 14.6G; CHOLESTEROL 10MG; SODIUM 529MG; CARBOHYDRATE 26.6G.

60 MINUTES

Southern Barley, Ham & Greens Soup

The earthy sweetness and hearty texture unique to barley can be coaxed to delicious perfection in many ways. But it's in this southern-inspired soup—loaded with lean ham and leafy greens—that those wonderful qualities really shine. If the soup becomes too thick, just add a bit more broth or water and adjust the seasonings to taste.

1	TABLESPOON OLIVE OIL	1	28-OUNCE CAN DICED TOMATOES, UNDRAINED
1½	CUPS CHOPPED ONION		
1½	CUPS PEELED AND CHOPPED CARROTS	5	CUPS (PACKED) COARSELY CHOPPED COLLARD GREENS (OR OTHER GREENS, SUCH AS SWISS CHARD)
4	CLOVES GARLIC, MINCED		
2½	TEASPOONS GROUND CUMIN		
8	CUPS LOW-SODIUM CHICKEN OR VEGETABLE BROTH	2	CUPS DICED LEAN HAM
		1	TABLESPOON HOT SAUCE, MORE OR LESS TO TASTE
1⅓	CUPS PEARL BARLEY		

Heat the oil in a large saucepan set over medium-high heat. Add the onion and carrots. Season with salt and pepper. Cook and stir 8 minutes. Add the garlic and cumin. Cook and stir 1 minute.

Add the broth and barley. Bring to a boil. Reduce the heat to medium low. Partially cover and cook 35 minutes, until the barley is tender.

Stir in the tomatoes with their juices and greens. Cover and simmer 5 to 6 minutes, until the greens are tender. Stir in the ham and hot sauce. Season the soup with salt and pepper to taste. **Makes 8 servings.**

Vegetarian Option: Prepare as directed, substituting 2 cups diced smoked tofu for the ham.

NUTRITION PER SERVING:
CALORIES 206; FAT 6.8G (SAT 2.4G, MONO 2.3G, POLY 2.0G);
PROTEIN 16.8G; CHOLESTEROL 76MG; SODIUM 679MG; CARBOHYDRATE 26.4G.

60
MINUTES

Wild Rice & Corn Soup

WITH CAJUN SPICES

A little sausage goes a long way in this earthy, supremely comforting soup. Look for whole wild rice grains; they cook more evenly and keep their nutty-chewy texture better than split or broken grains do.

6½ CUPS LOW-SODIUM CHICKEN BROTH, DIVIDED USE	1¼ CUPS CHOPPED ONION
⅔ CUP WILD RICE	1¼ CUPS PEELED AND CHOPPED CARROTS
3½ CUPS FROZEN (THAWED) CORN KERNELS, DIVIDED USE	1 TEASPOON EACH: DRIED THYME, BASIL, OREGANO, AND CUMIN
1 TABLESPOON CANOLA OIL	¼ TEASPOON CAYENNE PEPPER
¼ OF A 16-OUNCE PACKAGE LIGHT SMOKED SAUSAGE, CHOPPED	¾ CUP CANNED FAT-FREE EVAPORATED MILK (FROM A 12-OUNCE CAN)
	¼ CUP CHOPPED FRESH CHIVES

Place 2½ cups of the broth in a medium saucepan set over medium-high heat. Bring to a boil. Add the wild rice. Reduce the heat to medium low, cover, and cook 40 minutes, until the liquid evaporates and the rice is almost tender, stirring occasionally.

Meanwhile, place 2 cups of the corn and 1 cup of the remaining broth in a blender. Purée until smooth. Heat the oil in a large saucepan set over medium-high heat. Add the sausage, onion, and carrots. Cook and stir 5 minutes. Add the thyme, basil, oregano, cumin, and cayenne. Cook and stir 1 minute.

Add remaining 3 cups broth. Bring the soup to a boil. Reduce the heat to low and simmer the soup 15 minutes.

Add the cooked wild rice, corn purée, and the remaining 1½ cups corn kernels to soup. Cook until wild rice is very tender and flavors blend, about 15 minutes. Mix in the evaporated milk. Season with salt and pepper to taste. Serve garnished with the chives. **Makes 6 servings.**

Vegetarian Option: Prepare as directed, but substitute vegetable broth for the chicken broth and eliminate the sausage. Add ¾ cup diced smoked tofu at the same time as the evaporated milk.

NUTRITION PER SERVING:
CALORIES 213; FAT 6.8G (SAT 2.5G, MONO 2.1G, POLY 2.0G);
PROTEIN 8.3G; CHOLESTEROL 27MG; SODIUM 346MG; CARBOHYDRATE 35.3G.

60 MINUTES

Thai Coconut & Jasmine Rice Soup

Jasmine rice has a pleasant aroma that underscores the other Asian ingredients, but any long grain white rice will work. Eight ounces frozen, thawed medium shrimp, peeled and deveined, can be substituted for the tofu.

1	CUP UNCOOKED JASMINE RICE	1	SERRANO CHILE, SLICED INTO ROUNDS
2	14-OUNCE CANS LIGHT UNSWEETENED COCONUT MILK	2	TEASPOONS THAI RED CURRY PASTE
		2	TEASPOONS SUGAR
4	CUPS LOW-SODIUM CHICKEN OR VEGETABLE BROTH	¾	OF A 14- TO 16-OUNCE PACKAGE EXTRA-FIRM TOFU, DRAINED AND FINELY DICED
2	CUPS THINLY SLICED MUSHROOMS	½	CUP THINLY SLICED GREEN ONIONS
1	TABLESPOON GRATED LEMON ZEST	⅓	CUP THINLY SLICED BASIL
3	TABLESPOONS ASIAN FISH SAUCE (NAAM PLA)	3	TABLESPOONS FRESH LIME JUICE
3	TABLESPOONS PEELED AND MINCED FRESH GINGER	½	CUP FRESH CILANTRO LEAVES

Prepare the jasmine rice according to package directions.

While the rice cooks, combine the coconut milk, broth, mushrooms, lemon zest, fish sauce, ginger, chile, curry paste, and sugar in a large saucepan set over medium-high heat. Bring to a boil. Reduce the heat to medium low. Cover and simmer 10 minutes to blend flavors.

Add the tofu, green onions, basil, lime juice, and cooked rice. Cook 5 minutes longer to blend flavors. Season with salt and pepper to taste. Serve topped with the cilantro leaves. **Makes 6 servings.**

Vegetarian Option: Substitute soy sauce or liquid amino seasoning (e.g., Bragg Liquid Aminos) for the fish sauce.

NUTRITION PER SERVING:
CALORIES 167; FAT 6.1G (SAT 1.3G, MONO 3.2G, POLY 1.5G);
PROTEIN 13G; CHOLESTEROL 35MG; SODIUM 318MG; CARBOHYDRATE 14.1G.

45 MINUTES

Edamame Succotash Soup

I developed this soup in the depths of winter, when I was craving something soothing and hearty, but fresh-tasting. The edamame cozies up to the sweet corn in a way that manages to be both new and familiar. You can add chicken or chicken sausages to make the soup even heartier, but I prefer it as it is. And in case you are wondering about "creamed" corn in a healthy recipe: There is no "cream" in creamed corn (at least not traditional canned varieties).

1 TABLESPOON OLIVE OIL	½ CUP FINELY CHOPPED FRESH FLAT-LEAF PARSLEY LEAVES, DIVIDED USE
2 CUPS CHOPPED ONION	
1 LARGE RED BELL PEPPER, SEEDED AND CHOPPED	8 CUPS LOW-SODIUM CHICKEN OR VEGETABLE BROTH
4 CLOVES GARLIC, MINCED	1½ CUPS FROZEN SHELLED EDAMAME
2½ TEASPOONS DRIED BASIL	1 15-OUNCE CAN CREAMED CORN
1½ TEASPOONS DRIED THYME	1½ CUPS FROZEN (THAWED) CORN KERNELS
½ TEASPOON FRESHLY CRACKED BLACK PEPPER	

Heat the oil in a large saucepan set over medium-high heat. Add the onion and bell pepper. Season with salt and pepper. Cook and stir 5 minutes. Add the garlic, basil, thyme, black pepper, and ¼ cup of the parsley. Cook and stir 4 minutes.

Add the broth and edamame. Bring to a boil. Reduce the heat to medium low, cover, and cook 10 minutes, until the edamame are tender.

Stir in the creamed corn and corn kernels. Cook 5 minutes to blend flavors. Season with salt and pepper to taste. Ladle the soup into bowls and sprinkle with the remaining parsley. **Makes 8 servings.**

NUTRITION PER SERVING:
CALORIES 198; FAT 6.7G (SAT 1.4G, MONO 2.3G, POLY 2.1G);
PROTEIN 9.1G; CHOLESTEROL 0MG; SODIUM 432MG; CARBOHYDRATE 36.2G.

45 MINUTES

Red Lentil Mulligatawny

The name of this highly seasoned Indian soup means "pepper water." Although most often made with chicken, this version gets its body from red lentils. The soup gets quite a kick from the combination of curry, ginger, cumin, and cayenne.

1 MEDIUM TART-SWEET APPLE, PEELED AND DICED	1 CUP DRIED SMALL RED LENTILS
1 TABLESPOON CHOPPED FRESH CILANTRO LEAVES	1 CUP CHOPPED ONION
	1 14-OUNCE CAN LIGHT COCONUT MILK
1 MEDIUM RED BELL PEPPER, SEEDED AND CHOPPED, DIVIDED USE	3 TABLESPOONS TOMATO PASTE
	2 TEASPOONS MILD CURRY POWDER
5 TEASPOONS FRESH LIME JUICE, DIVIDED USE	1 TEASPOON GROUND GINGER
3½ CUPS LOW-SODIUM CHICKEN OR VEGETABLE BROTH	½ TEASPOON GROUND CUMIN
	¼ TEASPOON CAYENNE PEPPER

Combine the apple, cilantro, half of the red bell pepper, and 3 teaspoons of the lime juice in a small bowl. Cover and chill.

Place the broth, lentils, onion, and the remaining bell pepper in a large saucepan set over medium-high heat. Bring to a boil. Cover and reduce heat to medium low. Simmer 20 minutes, until the lentils are very tender.

Working in batches, purée the soup in a blender until smooth. Return the soup to the saucepan and stir in the coconut milk, tomato paste, curry, ginger, cumin, and cayenne. Cook 10 minutes, stirring occasionally, to blend flavors. Stir in the remaining 2 teaspoons lime juice. Season with salt and pepper to taste. Serve topped with the apple mixture. **Makes 4 servings.**

NUTRITION PER SERVING:
CALORIES 280; FAT 5.9G (SAT 4.4G, MONO 0.1G, POLY 0.1G);
PROTEIN 10.6G; CHOLESTEROL 0MG; SODIUM 577MG; CARBOHYDRATE 42.4G.

45 MINUTES

Southwestern Black Bean & Rice Soup

Cumin and lime, together with the chipotle chiles in the salsa, give this oh-so-easy soup its southwestern flavor. With the addition of some fresh and flavorful toppings—avocado, cilantro, and sour cream—it's as beautiful as it is darn good.

3½ CUPS LOW-SODIUM CHICKEN OR VEGETABLE BROTH

¾ CUP UNCOOKED LONG GRAIN RICE

1 15-OUNCE CAN BLACK BEANS, RINSED AND DRAINED

1 16-OUNCE JAR THICK-AND-CHUNKY-STYLE CHIPOTLE SALSA

1 CUP FROZEN CORN KERNELS, UNTHAWED

1 TABLESPOON FRESH LIME JUICE

2 TEASPOONS GROUND CUMIN

2 GREEN ONIONS, CHOPPED

1 SMALL AVOCADO, PEELED AND DICED

¼ CUP REDUCED-FAT SOUR CREAM

Place the broth and rice in a large saucepan set over medium-high heat. Bring to a boil. Reduce the heat to low, cover, and cook 20 minutes or until the rice is done.

Stir in the beans, salsa, corn, lime juice, and cumin. Cook 5 minutes to blend the flavors. Season with salt and pepper to taste. Serve topped with the green onions, avocado, and sour cream. **Makes 4 servings.**

NUTRITION PER SERVING:
CALORIES 158; FAT 5.3G (SAT 1.5G, MONO 2.6G, POLY 0.5G);
PROTEIN 6.1G; CHOLESTEROL 5.0MG; SODIUM 664MG; CARBOHYDRATE 24.6G.

30 MINUTES

White Bean & Basil Soup

This is probably the simplest soup you've ever made from scratch: You just throw everything into the blender and whiz away. All that's left is some warming in a pan to blend the flavors and heat it through and a few crunchy croutons on top.

2 16-OUNCE CANS WHITE BEANS, SUCH AS CANNELLINI, DRAINED	2 LARGE GARLIC CLOVES, MINCED
2 CUPS LOW-SODIUM CHICKEN OR VEGETABLE BROTH	½ CUP PACKED FRESH BASIL LEAVES, DIVIDED USE
1 CUP GOOD-QUALITY BOTTLED MARINARA SAUCE	⅛ TEASPOON CAYENNE PEPPER
	1 CUP PURCHASED LARGE CROUTONS

Place the beans, broth, marinara sauce, garlic, ¼ cup of the basil, and cayenne in a blender. Purée until smooth.

Transfer the mixture to a large saucepan set over medium heat. Cook and stir 5 minutes to blend the flavors. Season with salt and pepper to taste.

Roll the remaining basil leaves into a cigar-shape roll. Cut crosswise into thin slivers. Serve the soup topped with the slivered basil and the croutons. **Makes 4 servings.**

NUTRITION PER SERVING:
CALORIES 157; FAT 4.3G (SAT 0.6G, MONO 2.6G, POLY 0.6G);
PROTEIN 8.1G; CHOLESTEROL 0MG; SODIUM 758MG; CARBOHYDRATE 23.1G.

20 MINUTES

Split-Pea Soup

WITH CARAMELIZED ONIONS

Silky and sweet, caramelized onions add a sophisticated touch to this healthy and delicious soup.

1½ CUPS DRIED SPLIT YELLOW OR GREEN PEAS	4 CUPS LOW-SODIUM CHICKEN OR VEGETABLE BROTH
1 TEASPOON DRIED OREGANO LEAVES	1½ TABLESPOONS OLIVE OIL
½ TEASPOON CHIPOTLE CHILE POWDER	3 CUPS CHOPPED ONION
2 BAY LEAVES	1½ TEASPOONS WHOLE CUMIN SEEDS
2 CUPS WATER	

Place the peas, oregano, chipotle chile, bay leaves, water, and broth in a large saucepan set over high heat. Bring to a boil. Reduce heat to medium low and simmer, partially covered, 35 minutes, until the peas are tender. Discard the bay leaves.

Meanwhile, heat the oil in a heavy, large skillet set over medium-high heat. Add the onion. Cook and stir 20 minutes, until the onion is a deep golden brown.

Transfer half of the soup (mostly solids) to a blender. Purée until smooth. Return to the pan with the remaining soup and stir in the cumin seeds. Season with salt and pepper to taste. **Makes 6 servings.**

NUTRITION PER SERVING:
CALORIES 233; FAT 3.5G (SAT 1.1G, MONO 1.6G, POLY 0.5G);
PROTEIN 13.7G; CHOLESTEROL 4MG; SODIUM 456MG; CARBOHYDRATE 38.7G.

60 MINUTES

Quinoa & Garden Vegetable Soup

Once a revered food staple of the ancient Incans, quinoa (pronounced keen-wah) is packed with high-quality protein. In fact, at as much as 20 percent protein, it has more protein than any other whole grain. Add to that a good dose of B vitamins, iron, calcium, potassium, magnesium, and vitamin E, and it's easy to see why quinoa flies out of the bulk bins at health-food stores. But I know what you're thinking: What about the taste? Well, it's absolutely delicious. It's a mild, slightly sweet grain with hints of corn, nuts, and grass. It's a perfect complement to the garden vegetables in this soup. Though cooking quinoa is as easy as cooking rice, it does require one essential step: a good rinsing. Rinsing rids it of its coating of saponin, a bitter, soapy-tasting natural substance that protects the plant from insects and birds. Most quinoa is processed to remove much of the saponin, so submersion and a good swishing in a bowl of cool water is all it takes to finish the process. You can find quinoa in health-food stores and many supermarkets.

1 TABLESPOON OLIVE OIL	5 CUPS LOW-SODIUM CHICKEN OR VEGETABLE BROTH
1 CUP CHOPPED ONION	¼ CUP CANNED TOMATO PASTE
1 MEDIUM RED BELL PEPPER, SEEDED AND CHOPPED	1 CUP QUINOA, RINSED
5 CLOVES GARLIC, MINCED	1 14.5-OUNCE CAN DICED TOMATOES, UNDRAINED
3 LARGE CARROTS, PEELED, HALVED LENGTH-WISE AND THINLY SLICED CROSSWISE	1 15-OUNCE CAN WHITE NAVY BEANS, RINSED AND DRAINED
½ POUND GREEN BEANS, TRIMMED, CUT INTO 2-INCH LENGTHS	2 CUPS LOOSELY PACKED FRESH BASIL LEAVES
2 MEDIUM ZUCCHINI, HALVED LENGTHWISE AND SLICED CROSSWISE	OPTIONAL: FRESHLY GRATED PARMESAN CHEESE

Heat the oil in a large saucepan set over medium heat. Add the onion and bell pepper. Season with salt and pepper. Cook and stir 5 minutes. Add the garlic, carrots, green beans, and zucchini. Cook and stir 2 minutes longer.

Add the broth, tomato paste, and quinoa to the pan. Bring to a boil. Reduce the heat to medium low and simmer, partially covered, 30 minutes.

Add the tomatoes with their juices and beans. Cook 5 minutes to heat through. Season with salt and pepper to taste. Just before serving, stir in the basil leaves. If desired, sprinkle with the Parmesan cheese. **Makes 8 servings.**

NUTRITION PER SERVING:
CALORIES 182; FAT 4.2G (SAT 0.6G, MONO 2.1G, POLY 1.1G);
PROTEIN 7.1G; CHOLESTEROL 5.2MG; SODIUM 259MG; CARBOHYDRATE 28.6G.

60 MINUTES

Risotto Primavera Soup

An Italian classic, reinterpreted as a springtime soup. And like recipes for risotto, you can use this as a template recipe and make endless variations using the vegetables, herbs, and spices you prefer or have on hand. If you don't have the dry white wine, you can use an equal amount of broth in its place.

1 TABLESPOON OLIVE OIL	OPTIONAL: GENEROUS PINCH OF SAFFRON
2 CUPS CHOPPED ONION	2 CUPS (1-INCH) SLICED ASPARAGUS
JUICE AND GRATED ZEST OF 1 LARGE LEMON	(ABOUT 1 POUND)
¾ CUP ARBORIO RICE	1 CUP FROZEN PETITE PEAS, UNTHAWED
½ CUP DRY WHITE WINE	½ CUP FRESHLY GRATED FRESH PARMESAN
5 CUPS LOW-SODIUM CHICKEN OR	CHEESE
VEGETABLE BROTH	

Heat the oil in a large saucepan set over medium high heat. Add the onion. Season with salt and pepper. Cook and stir 2 minutes. Add the lemon juice, zest, and rice. Cook and stir 3 minutes.

Stir in the wine. Cook and stir 2 minutes, until almost completely absorbed. Stir in the broth and (optional) saffron. Bring to a boil. Reduce heat to low, cover, and simmer 12 minutes.

Stir in asparagus and peas. Cook, uncovered, 2 minutes or until the asparagus is crisp-tender. Season with salt and pepper to taste. Serve immediately, sprinkled with the Parmesan cheese. **Makes 4 servings.**

NUTRITION PER SERVING:
CALORIES 297; FAT 4.1G (SAT 0.6G, MONO 1.9G, POLY 1.4G);
PROTEIN 7.4G; CHOLESTEROL 5.7MG; SODIUM 233MG; CARBOHYDRATE 25.6G.

30 MINUTES

SOUPS BY TOTAL TIME

20-MINUTE SOUPS

Beef & Snow Pea Soup, 131

Chicken & Couscous Soup with Exotic
    Spices, 89

Chinese Shrimp & Egg Drop Soup, 111

Chinese-Style Bok Choy & Mushroom Soup,
    61

Crab, Tomato & Basil Bisque, 107

Curried Couscous, Spinach, and Roasted
    Tomato Soup, 57

Garlicky Spinach & Tomato Soup with
    Cheese Ravioli, 56

Golden Turkey Soup with Corn & Orzo, 90

Home-style Chicken Soup, 71

Roasted Red Bell Pepper & Parmesan Bisque
    with Shrimp, 112

Shrimp & Scallop Verde Posole, 110

Smoky Chili-Beef Soup, 128

Tortilla Chicken Soup, 79

Vegetable Tortellini Soup with Asparagus,
    Peas & Parmesan, 66

West African Spicy Chicken & Peanut Soup,
    83

White Bean & Basil Soup, 164

30-MINUTE SOUPS

Artichoke & Blue Cheese Bisque, 34

Asian Beef Noodle Soup with Cinnamon &
    Anise, 130

Asian Chicken Noodle Soup, 81

Asparagus Soup with Spring Herb Gremolata,
    33

Avgolémono (Greek Lemon & Rice Soup),
    148

Cajun Chicken & Vegetable Soup, 73

Carrot Soup with Cilantro-Lemon
    Chimichurri, 28

Cassoulet Soup, 142

Chicken Posole, 78

Classic Tomato Soup, 19

Coconut Shrimp Soup, 109

Corn & Crab Chesapeake Chowder, 113

Cream of Broccoli Soup, 20

Cream of Mushroom Soup, 24

Curried Black-Eyed Pea Soup, 152

Dijon Vegetable Chowder, 46

Fisherman's Chowder, 115

Garlic Soup with Poached Eggs & Ham, 136

Gingered Chicken & Vegetable Soup, 82

Gingered Fish & Watercress Soup, 98

60-Minute Soups

REFRESHING SOUPS FOR SPRING AND SUMMER

VEGETARIAN AND VEGAN SOUPS

Vegan Soups

ESPECIALLY LOW-CALORIE SOUPS

(175 CALORIES OR LESS)

Artichoke & Blue Cheese Bisque, 34

Asparagus Soup with Spring Herb Gremolata, 33

Avgolémono (Greek Lemon & Rice Soup), 148

Bean & Bacon Soup, 154

Beef & Snow Pea Soup, 131

Big-Batch Vegetable Soup, 43

Black Bean Soup with Pumpkin, Lime & Chipotle, 147

Butternut Squash Soup with Sage & Thyme, 23

Carrot Soup with Cilantro-Lemon Chimichurri, 28

Cauliflower Bisque with Apples & Indian Spices, 35

Chilled Honeydew-Cucumber Soup, 38

Chinese Hot & Sour Soup, 64

Chinese Shrimp & Egg Drop Soup, 111

Chinese-Style Bok Choy & Mushroom Soup, 61

Classic Tomato Soup, 19

Cold Avocado Soup with Smoky-Cilantro Cream, 37

Crab, Tomato & Basil Bisque, 107

Cream of Broccoli Soup, 20

Cream of Mushroom Soup, 24

Curried Black-Eyed Pea Soup, 152

Curried Couscous, Spinach, and Roasted Tomato Soup, 57

Dijon Vegetable Chowder, 46

Down Island Sweet Potato Bisque, 36

Garden Gazpacho, 39

Gnocchi Soup with Root Vegetables, Lemon & Dill, 63

Green Chile Chowder, 67

Hominy, Tomato & Chile Soup, 60

Irish Cabbage Soup, 45

Leek and Potato Soup, 21

Manhattan Clam Chowder, 114

Mushroom, Barley & Bacon Soup, 149

Petite Pea Soup with Crumbled Goat Cheese, 29

Pumpkin Soup, 30

Punjabi Potato & Cauliflower Soup with Minted Yogurt, 58

Roasted Red Bell Pepper & Parmesan Bisque with Shrimp, 112

Roasted Red Pepper Soup, 32

Shrimp & Scallop Verde Posole, 110

Southeast Asian Fish Soup, 100

Southwestern Black Bean & Rice Soup, 163

Spring Spinach Soup with Fresh Mint Cream, 22

Summer Corn & Basil Bisque, 31

Thai Coconut & Jasmine Rice Soup, 160

Thai Hot & Sour Soup with Shrimp, Ginger & Lime, 105

Watermelon Gazpacho, 40

West African Peanut Soup, 156

White Bean & Basil Soup, 164

Wild Mushroom Soup, 48

Winter Minestrone with Fennel, Chard & Potatoes, 53

Winter Vegetable Bisque with Sherry & Thyme, 27

Zucchini & Spinach Soup with Lemon & Feta, 25

ESPECIALLY LOW-FAT SOUPS

(5 GRAMS OF FAT OR LESS)

Asparagus Soup with Spring Herb Gremolata, 33

Avgolémono (Greek Lemon & Rice Soup), 148

Bean & Bacon Soup, 154

Big-Batch Vegetable Soup, 43

Black Bean Soup with Pumpkin, Lime & Chipotle, 147

Butternut Squash Soup with Sage & Thyme, 23

Caribbean Pepper Pot, 117

Carrot Soup with Cilantro-Lemon Chimichurri, 28

Cauliflower Bisque with Apples & Indian Spices, 35

Chilled Honeydew-Cucumber Soup, 38

Chinese Hot & Sour Soup, 64

Chinese Shrimp & Egg Drop Soup, 111

Chinese-Style Bok Choy & Mushroom Soup, 61

Classic Tomato Soup, 19

Corn & Crab Chesapeake Chowder, 113

Country Captain Soup, 84

Cream of Broccoli Soup, 20

Cream of Mushroom Soup, 24

Curried Black-Eyed Pea Soup, 152

Dijon Vegetable Chowder, 46

Down Island Sweet Potato Bisque, 36

Dutch Farmer's Cheese & Vegetable Soup, 62

Enlightened Scotch Broth, 133

French Lentil Soup, 157

Gnocchi Soup with Root Vegetables, Lemon & Dill, 63

Green Chile Chowder, 67

Hearty Brown Rice, Spinach & Mushroom Soup, 145

Hominy, Tomato & Chile Soup, 60

Leek and Potato Soup, 21

Lemon Chicken Soup with Fresh Spinach & Pasta, 75

Manhattan Clam Chowder, 114

Pho Bo (Spicy Beef Vietnamese Noodle Soup), 127

Puerto Rican Ham Soup with Pigeon Peas & Sofrito, 140

Pumpkin Soup, 30

Punjabi Potato & Cauliflower Soup with Minted Yogurt, 58

Quinoa & Garden Vegetable Soup, 166

Red Beans & Rice Soup, 151

Risotto Primavera Soup, 167

Roasted Red Bell Pepper & Parmesan Bisque with Shrimp, 112

Roasted Red Pepper Soup, 32

Soupe au Pistou, 59

Southeast Asian Fish Soup, 100

Spanish Seafood Soup, 101

Spicy Sweet Potato & Coconut Soup, 65

Split-Pea Soup with Caramelized Onions, 165

Spring Spinach Soup with Fresh Mint Cream, 22

Summer Corn & Basil Bisque, 31

Swedish Yellow Split-Pea Soup with Ham & Fresh Dill, 141

Thai Hot & Sour Soup with Shrimp, Ginger & Lime, 105

Tuscan Bread Soup (Ribollita), 50

Watermelon Gazpacho, 40

White Bean & Basil Soup, 164

Wild Mushroom Soup, 48

Winter Minestrone with Fennel, Chard & Potatoes, 53

Winter Vegetable Bisque with Sherry & Thyme, 27

Zucchini & Spinach Soup with Lemon & Feta, 25

RECI PE INDEX